THE ADVENTURES OF BLAKE & MORTIMER
Based on the characters of EDGAR P. JACOBS

THE TESTAMENT OF WILLIAM S.

Script: Yves Sente • **Artwork: André Juillard**

Colours: Madeleine DeMille

9th CINEBOOK
The 9th Art Publisher

Original title: Le Testament de William S.
Original edition: © Editions Blake & Mortimer / Studio Jacobs (Dargaud – Lombard s.a.) 2016
by Yves Sente & André Juillard
www.dargaud.com
All rights reserved
English translation: © 2016 Cinebook Ltd
Translator: Jerome Saincantin
Editor: Lisa Morris
Lettering and text layout: Design Amorandi
Printed in Spain by EGEDSA
This edition first published in Great Britain in 2016 by
Cinebook Ltd
56 Beech Avenue
Canterbury, Kent
CT4 7TA
www.cinebook.com
A CIP catalogue record for this book
is available from the British Library
ISBN 978-1-84918-339-0

AS THIS AUGUST EVENING COMES TO A CLOSE, A BREATH OF WELCOME COOLNESS MAKES UP FOR THE MERCILESS BAKING THAT THE SUN HAS GIVEN LONDON ALL DAY. EVEN PETER PAN, FROM ATOP HIS BRONZE PEDESTAL IN KENSINGTON GARDENS, SEEMS TO REJOICE IN THE ARRIVAL OF NIGHT.

NOT FAR FROM THERE IN BAYSWATER ROAD, MEMBERS OF THE LONDON DIPLOMATIC SOCIETY ARE TAKING LEAVE OF EACH OTHER AFTER CELEBRATING THE ARRIVAL OF THEIR NEW GERMAN COLLEAGUE.

Donnerwetter!* This is a velcome party I von't forget in a hurry!

*BY THUNDER!

I did not realise how late it vas! I am goink to get a good ... a good... Ach! How do you say...?

It's 'a good telling-off', Hans.

My poor friend! Has the much-vaunted German authority fallen so low, then?

Go on, make fun of me! You obfiously hafen't met my vife. I vill cut across the park. It vill be faster.

Across the park? At this hour?

That's not very wise. Haven't you heard of those gangs of thugs roaming the area at night...?

Was?* Do you mean those ... those... Ach! Vat are they called again? I definitely drank too much, my friends...

They're called 'Teddy boys'. Idle hoodlums with no respect for anyone or anything. You should be careful.

*WHAT?

Pff! A handful of scally-vags dressed like girls aren't goink to scare me more than my vife! Let them come!

Pom Pom
Pom

Hello there, daddy-o! Are you lost? We'll be nice and show you the way out ... for the contents of your wallet. And your hat — I like that too...

?

1

Ach! Not a chance!

I don't appreciate being forced to get my Oxfords wet, daddy-o. Looks like the toll just went up...

After him!

All right, he's had it. Let's scatter. Meet me at the usual place tomorrow. I'll have new tip-offs.

TWENTY MINUTES LATER, THE GANG LEADER EXITS THE TUBE AT OXFORD CIRCUS...

OXFORD CIRCUS STATION

...AND CONTINUES ON FOOT...

...TO 165 OXFORD STREET, WHERE A JAZZ CLUB WITH AN ALREADY SCANDALOUS REPUTATION HAS JUST OPENED.

MARQUEE

Come here, Dickie! Just in time – we're skint!

Is this all you're bringing back when I tipped you off about a party full of defenceless old diplomats?! Is this a joke?

Don't be mad at us, my lord. They've increased the number of patrols, and the bourgeoisie are starting to be wary around Notting Hill...

More excuses! Out of my sight! I'll contact you when I have something more within your reach.

EARLY AFTERNOON THE NEXT DAY, INSIDE THE LONDON COUNTY COUNCIL CHAIRMAN'S OFFICE AT COUNTY HALL...

If I summoned you here, gentlemen, it's because this business is becoming a lot more serious than we thought.

4

SIR ISAAC HAYWARD IS JOINED BY CAPTAIN FRANCIS BLAKE, HEAD OF MI5, AS WELL AS GLENN KENDALL, CHIEF INSPECTOR AT SCOTLAND YARD.

...Ever since the Notting Hill riots, the reports of attacks by gangs of Teddy boys have increased sharply. And they no longer concern only Jamaican or Indian populations targeted out of basic racism. **No!**

More and more Londoners are being assaulted. Listen to this: 'Last night the new first secretary of the German Embassy was ambushed in Kensington Gardens'... Can you believe that? This could turn into a diplomatic crisis!

Some 'highly placed people' are beginning to wonder if these attacks may not be hiding an attempt to destabilise British authorities. Which is why we're calling upon MI5 and demanding full collaboration between your services. We expect prompt results. Have I made myself clear, gentlemen?

The chief inspector and I have already successfully worked together,* Sir Isaac. We'll get our teams together this very afternoon.

You can count on us, sir.

*SEE VOLUME 1: THE YELLOW M

AND IT'S ONLY IN THE EVENING THAT CAPTAIN BLAKE, AFTER A LONG MEETING WITH HIS POLICE COUNTERPARTS IN THE YARD, RETURNS HOME TO 99A PARK LANE.

Thank you, Sergeant.

Goodnight, Captain!

Evening, Mrs Benson. Evening Philip. I see you're going out tonight.

Good Lord! It completely slipped my mind, what with the latest events.

I thought we might walk there, but I'll call a cab instead. That'll give you an extra ten minutes to get changed.

We are going out, Francis! To the Royal Albert Hall. Tonight is the premiere of the new production of The Merchant of Venice! Have you forgotten Sarah Summertown's invitation?

LESS THAN 20 MINUTES LATER, THE TAXI ORDERED BY PROFESSOR MORTIMER STOPS IN FRONT OF THE ROYAL ALBERT HALL'S ENTRANCE...

...AND OUR TWO FRIENDS IMMEDIATELY RUSH IN...

...AS THE MUSIC ANNOUNCING THE OPENING OF THE FIRST ACT BEGINS PLAYING.

3

THE CURTAIN HAS JUST OPENED ON THE BEGINNING OF THE FIRST ACT AND A STREET OF VENICE, ALONG WHICH ANTONIO, SOLANIO AND SALARINO ARE WALKING...

In sooth, I know not why I am so sad; it wearies me...

...AND THE ACTORS START TO DECLAIM THE LINES OF THE MOST FAMOUS PLAYWRIGHT IN THE ENGLISH LANGUAGE: WILLIAM SHAKESPEARE.

...let the forfeit be nominated for an equal pound of your fair flesh, to be cut off and taken in what part of your body pleaseth me.

...The one of them contains my picture, prince: if you choose that, then I am yours withal.

...Well, while I live I'll fear no other thing so sore as keeping safe Nerissa's ring.

TWO AND A HALF HOURS LATER...

AFTER THE LAST ENCORE, THE GUESTS OF THE GALA RECEPTION MINGLE IN THE ROYAL RETIRING ROOM TO SHARE THEIR IMPRESSIONS OVER A GLASS OF CHAMPAGNE.

My friends, allow me to introduce my daughter Elizabeth McKenzie. She's finishing her master's in English Literature at Cambridge. My only regret is that her late father, my dear Robert, is no longer with us to share my pride.

My congratulations, miss. You combine charm and intelligence — I see why your mother is so proud.

You're too kind, Professor.

Friends, may I introduce you to Walter, Earl of Oxford, a great enthusiast of the works of William Shakespeare!

Thank you, Lord Auchentoshan. That said, I personally wouldn't go as far as to claim that these works were written by Shakesp...

SARAH POLITELY OFFERS HER HAND TO SIR WALTER UNDER THE WARY EYES OF HER FRIENDS, AS THE EARL AND THE NOVELIST ARE BOTH OBVIOUSLY ILL AT EASE.

Mrs Summertown... How do you do?

How do you do?

CLAIMING AN URGENT MEETING, SIR WALTER AVOIDS FURTHER PRESENTATIONS AND HURRIEDLY RETREATS.

Goodness! What the devil got into that fellow?

I don't understand. I assure you it's the first time I've ever seen him behave in such a ... cavalier manner.

SUDDENLY SIR WALTER SEEMS TO FREEZE AS HE DISCOVERS THE PRESENCE OF SARAH SUMMERTOWN.

Sir Walter?!

It's not your fault, my dear. Much against my will, I happen to be the sole cause of this ridiculous situation.

The Earl of Oxford is the current leader of the self-styled 'Oxford-ians', who for almost 200 years have claimed, with supporting studies, that William Shakespeare the playwright never existed...

Shakespeare never existed?! How so?

The Oxford Lodge is trying to prove that a poor provincial from Stratford-upon-Avon could never have written such a genius body of work as signed by William Shakespeare.

I, on the other hand, happen to be the president of the William Shakespeare Defenders' Society — its great rival — whose goal is to keep those very works alive ... and defend their creator's honour! As you can imagine, the Earl doesn't like me very much...

Now, please accept our apologies... I invited dear Nastasia for the weekend so that she could meet my daughter. I foresee many long conversations that are boring for men!

What? Surely you don't mean to return to your cottage so late in the day!

No, don't worry. Actually I stay in accommodation above our Society's offices. It's not far from here, in Princes Gate. A short walk in the fresh air will do us good after all this entertainment.

With those gangs of Teds roaming around the park, letting you walk alone is out of the question, ladies! Philip and I will escort you.

As for me, I must take my leave here. I do apologise.

No need, Sir Archibald. Two bodyguards of the professor and captain's calibre will be more than enough. Than you for coming. Safe trip home.

5

THE SMALL PARTY WALK ALONG KENSINGTON ROAD TOWARDS PRINCES GATE...

...AND SOON ARRIVE AT THE BUILDING HOUSING THE OFFICES OF THE WILLIAM SHAKESPEARE DEFENDERS' SOCIETY.

ON THE WAY BACK, THE PROFESSOR AND THE CAPTAIN DECIDE TO MAKE THE BEST OF THE BALMY SUMMER NIGHT AND SMOKE A NICE PIPE.

MEANWHILE, ACROSS FROM THE ROYAL ALBERT HALL, A GANG OF PREDATORS HAVE LOCATED THEIR PREY...

That Shylock character! What a strange idea Shakespeare had, making him demand—

Shhh! Did you hear that?

?!

Let go of me, you thug!

Hooligan!

Hold on!

Help! Heeeelp!

Someone's in danger!

Francis! Look out!

By Saint Edward! These two fellows will...

Forget it! Everyone scatter!!

Philip! Go back to Park Lane and call Inspector Kendall! I'll see you there after I try and catch one of those scoundrels!

Right you are, Francis.

Oh dear!

As for you, my lad...

...don't think you can get away from me!

SOON THE TWO MEN ARE CROSSING THE BRIDGE OVER THE SERPENTINE.

NOT FAR FROM THE PARK'S EXIT, THE FUGITIVE LOOKS BACK IN AN ATTEMPT TO SEE HOW CLOSE HIS PURSUER IS — THE WRONG MOVE, IT TURNS OUT, AS HE TRIPS AND FALLS...

!

?

Dammit, where is it?

SEEING HIS HUNTER CLOSE IN, THE LEADER OF THE TEDDY BOYS HAS NO CHOICE BUT TO RUN AGAIN...

Blast it! This one's still pretty spry for a man of his age!

A MINUTE LATER, BLAKE, EXITING THE PARK ON THE VERGE OF EXHAUSTION, SEES HIS QUARRY TURN INTO HYDE PARK GARDENS.

REACHING THE CORNER, THE CAPTAIN FINDS THE STREET EMPTY.

?!

WELL AWARE THAT HE WON'T BE ABLE TO INSPECT EVERY BUILDING IN THE STREET ALONE, BLAKE DECIDES TO DOUBLE BACK...

...TOWARDS THE SPOT WHERE THE FUGITIVE HAD STUMBLED.

Why would he have wasted any time here unless...

...he'd dropped something? So this was it!

SHORTLY BEFORE MIDNIGHT, BLAKE IS BACK AT THE PARK LANE FLAT HE SHARES WITH MORTIMER.

We've had several victims claiming they'd been bludgeoned with canes that have animal heads.

Hmm. This one appears somewhat too finely wrought to belong to a mere mugger...

We should go to bed and sleep on it.

7

A LITTLE EARLIER THAT SAME EVENING, IN VENICE, A RECEPTION WAS HELD AT THE HOME OF THE MARQUIS STEFANO DA SPIRI.

Welcome, dear friends. I am delighted to have you as my guests here, in this family palace that has seen so many noble visitors over the centuries.

With your permission, I will begin with a round of introductions ... even though some of you have been friends for years.

To my right, my American friend Peggy Newgold. Next to her, Sir Russell Winson and his wife Lady Penelope, who have come for the screening of their new film at la Mostra.*

So you managed to avoid the air traffic controllers' strike?

Barely! Our flight was the last one to leave London.

To the right of Lady Penelope, Earl Arthur and Countess Abigail of Chatham — I believe you all know them.

Maria Vergine!** What are you doing?! We're going to hit! Hard to starboard!!!

I... I can't, Captain! The helm's not responding...

However, not all of you have met my friend Marcello Lamberti, a brilliant jeweller and watchmaker, and his charming wife Clara, a pianist.

Engines at full reverse to soften the blow! Brace for impact!

And finally, my friends Karl and Eva von Richentaus. They too came to attend the film festival ... before going to enjoy a second honeymoon in Tuscany.

Welcome one and all. My dearest wish is that this night will remain one of your best memories of Venice — as it will for me, I have no doubt.

And now, let us have dinn—

BAAAM

*LA MOSTRA INTERNAZIONALE D'ARTE CINEMATOGRAFICA — VENICE INTERNATIONAL FILM FESTIVAL. FOUNDED IN 1932, IT IS THE OLDEST IN THE WORLD.
**GOOD HEAVENS!

NOT TEN MINUTES LATER, THE VENETIAN POLICE HAVE ARRIVED.

AFTER EVALUATING THE SITUATION, SALMAN, MARQUIS DA SPIRI'S BUTLER, REPORTS TO HIS EMPLOYER.

...and fortunately, no one was injured. The police are bringing a tug to take the ship to the harbour.

Thank you, Salman. That's a relief.

You were hoping we'd never forget this night — I can assure you that your wish has been granted, my dear.

I thought the mad stuff only happened in Venice during the Carnevale!*

Did you perhaps arrange for this accident just to spice up your dinner a little, Marquis? I wouldn't put it past you.

I would never stoop to endangering this ancient palazzo. It's over five centuries old, and I treat it with more respect than those insufferable ships full of tourists do, believe me.

SOON PEACE HAS RETURNED TO THE PALAZZO DA SPIRI, WHERE LIGHT, CULTIVATED CONVERSATIONS HAVE RESUMED...

...UNTIL SOME 20 MINUTES LATER, WHEN A LONG, DULL SOUND APPEARS TO RISE FROM THE BOWELS OF THE BUILDING.

Bonggg!

Bonggg!

What on earth...? It sounds like ... a bell?!

How mournful... What is it?

Bonggg!

By Jupiter, Salman! What is this noise?

I do not know, Marquis. The tug has taken the damaged ship away, so it can't be...

Actually, the sound is coming from inside the palace, sir. From the cellar, I would say...

Bonggg!

By the devil, you're right! Let's listen carefully...

Bonggg!

Bonggg!

I do apologise, my friends, but I must go and find out what is so inopportunely disrupting our dinner.

I'm going with you!

Me too!

Bonggg!

I would love to see the cellars of such a palace! I'm coming too!

I'm far too intrigued not to follow!

Oh yes! This is all so much fun! Let's all go!

*CARNEVALE DI VENEZIA – CARNIVAL OF VENICE. AN ANNUAL FESTIVAL FAMOUS FOR ITS ELABORATE COSTUMES AND MASKS.

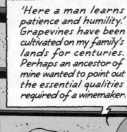

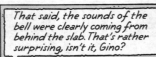

*TRADITIONALLY, FRENCH THEATRES ANNOUNCE THE BEGINNING OF A PERFORMANCE WITH A SERIES (OFTEN NINE) OF SHARP RAPS OF A WOODEN STAFF ONTO THE STAGE, ENDING IN THREE SLOWER ONES JUST BEFORE THE CURTAIN RISES.
**EXCELLENCY, MY LORD...

There's a space back here. Salman, we need torches.

I'm scared, Marcello. I won't go any further!

Calm down, darling.

I suggest the ladies go back upstairs to wait for us. This expedition might prove more dangerous than anticipated...

There's no way I'm going back, Sir Russell!

This is all too exciting. I'm staying too!

Come, dear. We'll go and have a little pick-me up in the library while our friends play explorers...

I'm too old for such antics. Allow me to escort you, ladies.

Here are the torches, Marquis.

Well! Let's see what's hiding behind this slab...

QUI L'UOMO IMP LA PAZIEN E L'UMIII

?!

Good heavens! So this is where the sounds came from?! A bell rung by some sort of clockwork mechanism ... just like the one that opened the passage...

This is insane! What's the meaning of this setup?!

There a spiral staircase here, Marquis. Perhaps our questions will be answered further down.

WHEN THE MARQUIS AND HIS FRIENDS, HAVING DESCENDED SEVERAL FEET, COME TO ANOTHER SECRET CHAMBER, THEY ARE THE FIRST...

...TO DISCOVER THE INCREDIBLE SIGHT THAT'S BEEN WAITING FOR OVER THREE CENTURIES.

11

UNDER THE EMPTY GAZE OF THE DUMMY IMPRISONED IN ITS GLASS CAGE, THE MARQUIS PICKS UP THE DOCUMENTS RESTING ON THE LECTERN.

HAVING UNSEALED THE LETTER, STEFANO DA SPIRI BEGINS TO READ IT...

Well, Marquis? What does the letter say? We are all agog!...

Let's join the others in the library, my friends. We're all going to need that pick-me up.

Please excuse the quality of my translation. My Latin has become somewhat rusty over the years...

'Venice, 25 August 1632... Dear friends and eminent members of our Mind Gamesters brotherhood, with the posthumous blessing of my friend and brother from Stratford, I, Guglielmo da Spiri, have invited you tonight to participate in one of our bouts of mental jousting for the final time.

The prize will be the discovery of the truth about the great William Shake-Speares. Whoever among you manages to bring together the three keys of knowledge shall have access to the supreme reward ... the unpublished play from the 'Double Master'. Once you have succeeded in this quest, you will understand why I must protect my family's name, forever hidden behind that of William S.

'With this letter I leave the first part of the story that will shed light on my double life. This first chapter concludes with a little riddle whose solution will lead the most subtle among you to the first key and the second part of the story. So shall it be for the third and last part.

'I wish you a happy investigation, my friends, and may the best man win! We will meet again in another world, one that I hope will be to our taste and where together we will celebrate the man who honoured me by calling me his Fair Lord. Your humble servant, Guglielmo da Spiri, Marquis of Venezia.'

That's all the letter says. The leather satchel contains what seems to be the beginning of an autobiography.

This is strange. Your ancestor wrote this letter to guests of his time who never received it. Why is it revealed to us so long afterwards?!

What's truly incredible is that it mentions Shakespeare and, if I understood correctly, a play that's ... as yet unknown!?...

My ancestor was equally passionate about sciences and the arts. The works of Leonardo da Vinci were as fascinating to him as that of Aristotle or Galileo.

Along with a few close friends, he'd created a sort of brotherhood of aesthetes, the 'Mind Gamesters', whose members regularly set intellectual challenges for each other. He's also remembered for having mysteriously disappeared in 1632, the day after a...

By all the...! I'm sure it was...

Yes, that's it! The testimony of my ancestor's butler. He recounts how, that evening of 1632, Guglielmo da Spiri had invited the members of his brotherhood to a sumptuous feast here, in this very palace.

'...Every invited guest came, but the master remained absent. Even I didn't know where he was. That evening, a mild earthquake shook the Serenissima*. As the marquis still didn't show, the visitors, worried about aftershocks, decided to return home...'

'...and no one ever heard from Marquis Guglielmo da Spiri again.'

An earthquake, you say? In that case, I may have an idea about what happened...

*A NAME FOR THE VENETIAN REPUBLIC, MEANING 'THE MOST SERENE'.

I believe the clockwork mechanism we saw was built to function on a timer. Let's assume that your ancestor wanted his guests to find what we discovered tonight. He wound up his device ... but had no way of planning for the earthquake!

The tremor probably caused minute rock falls that blocked the mechanism...

...and the shock caused by the ship colliding with the palace tonight released it – over three centuries later?!

Why not? The mechanism seemed to be ingenious and built with quality materials, which, in an atmosphere preserved from damp, wouldn't have degraded over the centuries.

It sounds like we have a technical explanation. That leaves one question: what shall we do with that 'testament'?!

We need to find a specialist on Shakespeare...

The name Sarah Summertown springs to mind. She's president of the William Shakespeare Defenders' Society, and I often consult with her when one of my films makes a reference to Shakespeare.

Sarah Summer....!?

What was her name again?

Sarah Summertown. Archaeologist, novelist and something of an adventurer. The press mentioned her recently after she returned from Africa.

I think I read something about that, yes...

It's an excellent suggestion, Sir Russell. Could you call her tomorrow? You can explain the situation and tell her that I will be sending my butler. Salman will bring her these new documents in person.

I insist on being informed of the outcome of this adventure, my dear!

So do I!

I promise, my friends. For the moment, though, I believe we have all had enough excitement. These documents are going to spend the night in this desk, and we ... in our beds! My people will show you to your rooms. Goodnight, all.

13

AN HOUR LATER THE MARQUIS, TROUBLED BY THE DAY'S EVENTS, STILL HASN'T FOUND SLEEP.

AS ALWAYS WHEN PLAGUED WITH INSOMNIA, HE SEEKS PEACE OF MIND IN HIS LIBRARY.

BUT THAT NIGHT, HE DOESN'T FIND IT TO BE HIS USUAL HAVEN OF PEACE.

?!

You're wasting your time with that letter opener. The lock on that drawer is old but quite sturdy. Come here and show me your face instead...

I'm warning you, I know how to use this. I advise you to...

Ow!

Ohhhhh...

THE PROJECTILE HAVING BOUNCED OFF HIS FOREHEAD, THE MARQUIS SOON REGAINS CONSCIOUSNESS...

Salman? Join me in the library, please... Yes, now. No, don't worry about changing...

Ah! I think it was in this magazine that...

'Sarah Summertown. Writer... and righter of wrongs!' Yes, this was it. Let's see...

LIFE

'Back from Africa with, as a trophy, the most wanted villain in the world!' That's her indeed. But... Well, I'll be! She knows him too?! What a coincidence... Yes.

Yes... It's him I should call!!

BOAC

16

A FEW MINUTES LATER...

...so I'd like you to post two men on guard at the door until tomorrow...

...then go back to bed. Tomorrow you'll take the first train to London. I won't feel safe until those documents have left the palace.

Crrrack...

!

Who... Is someone there?

Hmm... It'd be wise to make copies of all this before the morning.

AND WHILE THE MARQUIS BEGINS MAKING PHOTOCOPIES...

...SALMAN HAS AN UNEXPECTED ENCOUNTER...

Hey! You! One moment, please!

Herr von Richentaus?

Goodness, young fellow! Is it such a crime to want a little snack in the home of Marquis Da Spiri? Er... The kitchen is this way, right?

MEANWHILE, IN THE LIBRARY...

Crrrack!...

My, you're a bold one, my dear stranger!...

...This time, though... Oh! Abigail! I do apologise.

I'm sorry to bother you, my friend. I came to get a book that might help me sleep...

Insomnia, you say? How about re-reading A Midsummer's Night Dream by our esteemed William Shakespeare?

Or perhaps The Merchant of Venice, since we're in your wonderful city?

An excellent idea. You honour me, Countess. Sleep well, and have no fear. My people are keeping watch...

15

THE NEXT MORNING...

I hope you will remember our soirée fondly in spite of everything. The Chathams asked me to give you their apologies for leaving without proper goodbyes, but Sir Arthur had a professional appointment early this morning near the Piazza San Marco.

AS PLANNED, SIR RUSSELL WINSON CALLS THE OFFICES OF THE WILLIAM SHAKE-SPEARE DEFENDERS' SOCIETY TO ANNOUNCE SALMAN'S IMMINENT ARRIVAL.

That's right, Mr Spike. On the evening train, yes, since the strike in London's airports continues... Yes, with important documents... Please let Mrs Summertown know, will you?

Of course, Sir Russell. You can count on me. I will let her know the moment she arrives this morning.

Here are the documents, Salman. Needless to say, I urge you to take good care of them. And this one must be posted immediately.

I don't understand, sir. I'm leaving for London this morning...

...I could take this second package as well, rather than mailing it...

Tut- tut. Just be very careful and do as I ask. I have my reasons...

MEANWHILE, IN A LUXURY HOTEL IN VENICE...

Hello, London?... Connect me to the Oxford Lodge. Yes, in Belgrave Square...

Forgive me, Venerable Master. Brother De Vere insists on speaking to you urgently...

I'm listening, Brother De Vere...

Hmm... This is indeed very interesting... Yes. You were absolutely right to call. Keep abreast of events. I'll take care of the rest...

Good Lord! If this is true, it leaves us very little time... Apprentice, have my car readied.

Right away, Venerable Master.

I need someone both unscrupulous and with sufficient culture to be able to follow such a trail... Yes. I don't see anyone else but him. The problem being that... We'll see.

MOMENTS LATER, SIR WALTER LEAVES OXFORD LODGE.

It's all right, James, I won't need you today. I'm going to drive myself.

HE IMMEDIATELY PLUNGES INTO LONDON'S TRAFFIC TO HEAD TO THE DECIDEDLY LESS POSH NEIGHBOURHOOD...

...OF THE NOTORIOUS WANDSWORTH PRISON...

...WHERE SIR WALTER SEEMS TO HAVE PRIVILEGED ACCESS.

Here, and make sure we have the visiting room to ourselves for at least half an hour.

More than half an hour and it's extra, m'lord...

So, this is the infamous ... Colonel Olrik!

My name is Walter, Earl of Oxford. Delighted.

I wish I could say the same, but I don't know you...

I, on the other hand, know enough about your past history and network of henchmen to offer a ... highly profitable mission. If it is completed, it'll allow you to pay for your escape.

Interesting. Well, since you're here, I might as well listen to you...

17

THAT EVENING, THE TRAIN FROM VENICE ARRIVES IN LONDON...

...DEPOSITING MARQUIS DA SPIRI'S MESSENGER.

That's him. Go get the car. I'll meet you at the taxi stand.

Good evening. The corner of Kensington Road and Palace Gate, please!

You're as good as there already, sir!

WASTING NO TIME, THE BUTLER LEAVES THE STATION.

IMMEDIATELY, THE TWO MYSTERY MEN PULL OUT AFTER THE TAXI...

Get ready to put the pedal to the metal. We'll need to act as soon as possible.

No sign of a bobby. Go for it!

THE DRIVER GUNS THE ENGINE AND THE POWERFUL AMERICAN CAR SHOOTS AHEAD OF THE CAB...

...BEFORE FORCING IT TO STOP BY CUTTING IN FRONT OF IT.

Hand over your briefcase, quick! Or else...

Lord almighty!... What... What the devil just happened?!

The documents! Maria Vergine, this is terrible!

To Wandsworth — and hurry up! The senior guard gave us until 10.30 p.m. Otherwise the boss won't have the documents until tomorrow ... and we'll get an earful!

FIFTEEN MINUTES LATER, THE TAXI DROPS OFF HIS UNFORTUNATE PASSENGER.

Mr Spike? I'm Salman, Marquis Da Spiri's butler.

Please follow me. Mrs Summertown is waiting for you.

AFTER SOME QUICK INTRODUCTIONS, SALMAN INFORMS THE PRESIDENT OF THE SOCIETY THAT HE HAS JUST BEEN THE VICTIM OF AN ASSAULT AND THEFT...

My goodness, young man! That's quite a story! Considering the situation, I suggest...

...that we call the Marquis right away.

I was about to ask.

SUCCINCTLY, STEFANO DA SPIRI IS BROUGHT UP TO DATE.

Hmm. I see... No, don't say that, Salman. This isn't your fault... Very well. Let me speak to her.

...Yes, I think I understand, Marquis. Thank you for your trust... I'm going to call the captain immediately. He'll have the originals sent to me as soon as he gets them tomorrow... Yes, of course. The moment I know something new... Goodnight, Marquis.

Your employer gave me a quick description of his discovery. What's incredible is that these events have occurred precisely this year ... and at the end of August too!

What do you mean? How is the date relevant to any of this?

I have to check something important. But first of all...

SECONDS LATER, THE TELEPHONE RINGS IN THE LIVING ROOM OF 99A PARK LANE.

DRIING DRIING

IT DOESN'T TAKE LONG FOR THE PROFESSOR TO DETECT THE WORRY IN HIS FRIEND'S VOICE.

The captain? He's not here, but he shouldn't be much longer, and... I see... Why don't you come over with your visitor? We'll wait for him together... Excellent. I'll see you in a bit, then!

MEANWHILE, IN WANDSWORTH...

That's all there was, boss. Can't make head or tail of it — it's all gibberish...

Of course you can't, fool! It's Latin. I'm going to read this tonight. Come back tomorrow morning first thing.

19

TWENTY MINUTES LATER, THE TAXI ORDERED BY SARAH SUMMERTOWN IS HEADING TOWARDS PARK LANE WHEN ITS PATH IS BLOCKED BY A TRAFFIC ACCIDENT.

I'm afraid we're stuck here for a while!

THE WRITER QUICKLY DECIDES TO PAY THE FARE AND CONTINUE ON FOOT THROUGH HYDE PARK.

A greying lady and a Negro... Time to go to work, Dickie!

You can count on us, m'lord.

Come on, lads. Let's show that blackie he should have stayed in Notting Hill and make the lady pay for the bad company she's keeping...

Mrs Summertown! Look!

What in the...? If these are hooligans, they'll get a piece of my mind!

Sorry, Mrs Summertown, but we're not going to argue with five violent men armed with canes! Run! I'll hold them back.

Ouch!

Help! Help!

Ow!

Aaaah!

Mrs Summertown?!

Don't stop, you idiots! We need them!

Are you badly hurt?

It's my ankle...

Take the woman's handbag!

Oi! Let's dance, blackie! We'll teach you how to...

...the English way!

Hold it right there, my lad!

Your dance lessons will not take place in front of my house. On the other hand, if you don't scarper right now, I'll happily let you sample a few Scottish traditions.

Goodness gracious! Philip's under attack! David, with me!

By Saint George! Those two again!

Hold on, Philip! We're coming!

We're done! Scatter! Scatter!

Shall we pursue them, Captain?

No, David. Call Kendall and ask him to have the parks surrounded, even though I'm afraid it's already too late.

Hold on to my arm and let's go inside, Sarah. Mrs Benson will prepare us a tonic.

Excuse me. May I have a look at this cane, mister... Mister...?

Salman, sir. Here, it's all yours.

I'm Marquis Da Spiri's butler. He sent me to meet Mrs Summertown.

Stefano Da Spiri! I knew him very well, although we've lost touch since the talks between the Allies at the end of the Second World War! Do come in. You can tell us your reason for being here.

I'm going to call a doctor.

No need to bother a doctor at this hour, Philip. I already feel much better.

You need to put ice around the ankle. Leave it to me!

SOON, SALMAN RECOUNTS THAT STRANGE NIGHT IN VENICE, AS WELL AS THE ATTACK ON HIS CAB IN LONDON.

...The car was a big blue Ford, and the man who stole the briefcase had a strong American accent.

NEXT, SARAH ADDS WHAT SHE LEARNT FROM THE MARQUIS BEFORE THE EVENING'S LATEST EVENTS.

This all seems to be taking on disturbing proportions for a 'simple study of a historical text', no matter how rare and interesting it might be...

I'm afraid, Philip, that this isn't merely about an intellectual joust between scholars ...

21

Last night at the Royal Albert Hall, I mentioned the old rivalry between Stratfordians and Oxfordians. Well, now I need to give you a few more details about that...

Originating in the 19th century, the negationist theories became popular in 1920 with the publication of John Looney's *Shakespeare Identified*. This assigns the authorship of the works to Edward De Vere, 17th Earl of Oxford.

Looney considered that a provincial from Stratford could never have had such an astute and far-ranging knowledge of European cultures, and even less of the world of nobility, as was necessary to write his plays.

You have to admit that it's a remarkable state of affairs. Especially at a time when the vast majority of people never travelled.

We could debate the quality of education at the grammar school young Shakespeare attended in Stratford... But we must focus on another aspect of this whole situation — the financial one...

And that brings us back to the 19th century, and to a striking moment in London's history. I'm sure you've heard of the 'Great Stink' of 1858?

Summer was exceptionally hot that year. The level of the Thames lowered considerably. Soon, the smell from the stagnant waters became unbearable.

The authorities, worried about the spread of cholera, commissioned Joseph Bazalgette, chief engineer of the Metropolitan Board of Works, to effect a thorough cleaning of the sewer system, followed by its overhaul and extension.

Dozens of 'flushermen' were sent into action. Their job was to remove or flush away everything that might block the flow of water in the pipes.

A member of the team sent to the tunnels that ran between the old Globe Theatre foundations and the south bank of the Thames found a small coffer in the mud, left by the drop in water level.

Towards the end of August, chief engineer Joseph Bazalgette, inspecting the various objects found in the pipes, was intrigued by the coffer and opened it. Inside he found a mysterious, short handwritten text signed with a simple 'W.S.'...

That same evening he took the piece of parchment to his club and showed it to his friend Lord Lupus Sandfield, a fabulously wealthy member of London's real estate scene and renowned collector of ancient books and manuscripts.

I've read that text so often that I can recite it to you from memory!

'Guglielmo, my Fair Lord... How heartbroken I was to learn that you had been forced to leave. When will you and my sweet Dark Lady come back to me? In case we are fated never to meet again, I entrust you and the Serenissima with the task of leaving to posterity our last play, along with the truth about us, Shake-Speares.' And it's signed...

...'W.S, London, 29 June 1613.'

Sorry, Sarah, but you did say 'us, Shakespeares'?!

Yes, with a hyphen between 'Shake' and 'Speares'. It so happens that this spelling is the one that appears in the first edition of his sonnets, published in 1609. I have a facsimile...

Here, look!

Another crucial clue: the letter in the coffer was intended for a 'Fair Lord'. The same Fair Lord that Shakespeare addresses in most of his sonnets! Not to mention the 'Dark Lady' to whom 26 sonnets are dedicated!

SHAKE-SPEARES
SONNETS
Never before Imprinted.

AT LONDON
By G. Eld for T. T. and are
to be solde by william Aspley.
1609

Everything said in that letter coincides with the contents of the few historical documents available to historians. And let's not forget that the coffer was found where the Globe Theatre stood before it burnt down on 29 June 1613...

...the very day that this message was written and possibly placed in the coffer! A fascinating collection of coincidences.

One thing is certain. This letter tells us that in 1613 there existed an unknown play by the Bard! We named that mythical and still-elusive document *The Testament of William S.* But I haven't finished my story...

By the end of August 1858, when Lord Sandfield found himself in possession of the mysterious letter, the Stratfordians and Oxfordians had already been engaged in a merciless struggle within London's high society for almost half a century.

Two societies in particular were waging a bitter war. The Stratfordians of the William Shakespeare Defenders' Society...

...and the Oxfordians of the Temple of the Oxford Lodge. Each side manoeuvred to establish its truth within academic and literary circles...

...to the point that, more than once, heated debates escalated into duels, stupidly causing the death of supposedly intelligent and educated men.

23

Three of Lord Lupus Sandfield's friends had already been killed in those pointless duels that pitted the rival societies against each other. He then had an idea to stop such an absurd waste of human lives.

On 30 August, he sent simultaneous invitations to Earl Francis of Oxford and Sir Douglas Pulteney, leaders of the anti- and pro-Stratfordians respectively.

The two men came to Lord Sandfield's club at the appointed time and day — four o'clock, 1 September.

By Saint George! I thought this club was open only to men of culture!

More insults?! Well, here's a glove that'll...

Gentlemen! Please cease at once!

The gentlemen of London have had quite enough of your ridiculous conflict. So you're going to listen very carefully!

After showing his two guests the documents recovered from the sewers, Lord Sandfield exposed — and imposed — his 'peace plan'.

...In conclusion, here is the agreement that I am asking you to sign today, before my solicitor Mr Gilbert Bridges.

In exchange for your mutual promise to never fight a duel again — a binding promise for your descendants too — I vow to donate the sum of £100,000 to whichever of your two societies will first succeed in bringing absolute and written proof of the real authorship of William Shakespeare's works.

This offer will stand for **a hundred years** as of today at five o'clock, on condition that my descendants will maintain it. I sincerely hope so.

If they don't, or a century passes without proof, the offer will expire and the money will go to my heirs.

That was well played on the part of Lord Sandfield. I imagine he was hoping a century would be enough to bury old hatreds once and for all.

Exactly, Captain. And the plan worked!

The two societies vowed to respect the pact, and from that day there was never another duel between their members. However, no tangible proof of who truly authored Shakespeare's work was found either...

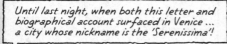

Until last night, when both this letter and biographical account surfaced in Venice ... a city whose nickname is the 'Serenissima'!

Not to mention that the letter and text were written by a certain Guglielmo Da ... Spiri... — the same first name as the one mentioned in the 1858 manuscript!

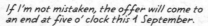

If I'm not mistaken, the offer will come to an end at five o'clock this 1 September.

And you're as aware as I am of today's date: 29 August 1958. And it's almost midnight...There's very little time left!

Unfortunately, since the only document that offered the beginning of a lead was stolen from Salman, how are we to...?

Well, as it happens, the marquis was quick to understand that he should be wary. He told me on the phone that Salman was only carrying copies...

He mailed the originals directly to his old friend in British intelligence... To you, Captain! You should receive them at your office tomorrow morning...

My goodness! I almost forgot!

I'll be right back.

Here. Any mail addressed to MI5 is delivered by special courier as soon as it reaches London. I brought what I didn't have time to open at the office with me, and I do believe that...

Yes! This must be it — this envelope came from Italy...

AT THE SAME INSTANT IN WANDSWORTH PRISON, ANOTHER TREASURE HUNTER IS PORING OVER THE COPIES OF THE VENICE DOCUMENTS...

Effigy... Effigy... The key is in that word. I'd stake my life on it. But no portrait of Shakespeare was ever made while he was alive...

So the 'effigy' would refer to... Yes! Of course!

25

Goodness gracious! This is it... The original of Guglielmo da Spiri's letter... and the first part of his autobiographical manuscript!

If those thieves work for the Oxford Lodge, I fear that, beyond any financial considerations, our opponents may be bent on destroying the discovery in order to preserve their image and the Lodge's raison d'être. That would be a disaster for the world's cultural heritage.

Let's start by contacting the solicitor in charge of the file. I believe the office of Bridges and Son is still in existence. Considering our time frame, I think you should call him right away. I'll give you a hand.

Mr Bridges? This is Sarah Summertown, president of the WSDS. I do apologise for calling you so late but I'm facing an extremely urgent situation...

THE DESCENDANT OF GILBERT BRIDGES CONFIRMS THAT LORD LUPUS SANDFIELD'S OFFER IS TECHNICALLY STILL VALID, AS NONE OF HIS HEIRS EVER CANCELLED IT AND THE CUT-OFF DATE HASN'T ARRIVED YET.

...It would be best if you came to see the original documents at my office tomorrow morning... Yes, eight o'clock is fine.

Good. Let's wait until morning. I'll ask Mrs Benson to prepare a couple of rooms. It'd be out of the question for you to go out again tonight.

MEANWHILE, THE SOLICITOR HAS PULLED THE OLD SANDFIELD FILE OUT OF A SAFE. HE IMMEDIATELY DECIDES TO CALL THE CURRENT HEAD OF THE NOBLE FAMILY...

...Yes, Lord Sandfield. I must see you urgently. Ideally tonight. This is about your financial future, I assure you.

My financial future, you say? All right, come at once. I'll let Jasper know...

His financial future?! This calls for close observation...

28

AT THIS LATE HOUR, THE SOLICITOR'S TAXI ONLY TAKES A FEW MINUTES TO TRAVEL FROM GROSVENOR SQUARE TO HYDE PARK GARDENS.

Good evening, Jasper. I'm sorry for keeping you up so late.

That's all right, Mr Bridges. Lord Sandfield is waiting for you in his office.

Well, Mr Bridges, I hope you're not here to tell me that my finances are doing even worse that I thought!

Maybe not, my lord. Maybe not...

THE SOLICITOR WASTES NO TIME IN RECOUNTING THE CALL HE RECEIVED FROM SARAH SUMMERTOWN...

...and, having checked, I must conclude that the offer remains entirely valid. At least until this 1 September at five o'clock precisely.

AS THE TWO MEN DISCUSS THE SITUATION, A THIN WOOD PANEL IN ONE OF THE WALLS SLIDES OPEN SLIGHTLY.

FROM INSIDE A NARROW SECRET HALLWAY IN THE OLD HOUSE, THE SPY HEARS EVERY WORD OF THE CONVERSATION.

...all of this to remind you of the origin of and reasons behind your ancestor's bequest... However, the will also contains a key clause that could restore your finances entirely. Listen...

'Should I die before evidence is found, I ask my descendants to respect my wishes until the end of the hundred years. That said, the decision to honour my decision will rest only with them, and each one will be free to either retrieve the reserved sum or to confirm the terms of this will with solicitors Bridges and Sons.'

This is unequivocally clear, my lord. If you choose not to prolong the will, the money will revert to you immediately. In which case, all your pecuniary problems would...

That's out of the question!

I beg your pardon, my lord?

You heard me right, Mr Bridges.

'...I ask my descendants to respect my wishes...' Lord Lupus isn't responsible for his heirs' bad financial luck. I shall therefore uphold his will and the family's honour. The matter is now closed ... until five o'clock on 1 September.

This decision does you credit, my lord.

That's it. It's clear now. The old man's gone totally mad!

27

29

PARK LANE, THE NEXT DAY...

Aaah!

Then you must stay in bed until the doctor's seen you. Salman will keep an eye on you if necessary...

But...

The professor's right, Mrs Summertown. Walking in your condition will only make things worse.

I'm also calling Mr Bridges to ask him if he can come to us instead.

Sarah!

It's all right. I tried to get up and... My ankle...

Don't worry. They'll both be here soon.

Thank you, Philip. While we wait for them, I'm going to give my daughter a call.

TWENTY MINUTES LATER...

...Further compounded by a torn ligament. It's essential for her to stay in bed for at least three weeks!

We'll see to it, Doctor.

THE DOCTOR HAS BARELY LEFT THE ROOM BEFORE THE SOLICITOR TAKES HIS PLACE.

...And, having checked, I can confirm that Lord Lupus Sandfield's will is still valid until five o'clock on 1 September!

I read in the papers that Lord Samuel Sandfield was currently having some financial difficulties...?

Indeed. But last night, in his home, he formally approved his ancestor's will, which he intends to see respected.

The words 'sense of honour' are as meaningful as ever to Lord Sandfield... Which isn't the case with the new generation. His son is rather more difficult to handle, if you know what I mean.

Hmm... By the way, how much are we talking about in today's money?

Taking into account the judicious investments made by Bridges and Son as well as the interests accrued over a century, we're looking at a sum of...

...nearly ten million pounds!

This Lord Sandfield is a true gentleman. If we find the documents in time, we'll find a financial arrangement that'll take his situation into account.

One problem at a time, though... I've just asked my daughter Elizabeth to take over this mission from me. She has the necessary skills.

Don't you think it could prove a dangerous adventure for that young lady? The attack on Salman has proved that...

I did think of that, Philip. Which is why I also thought of you...

Of me?!...

SARAH SUMMERTOWN HAS NO TROUBLE CONVINCING HER OLD FRIEND MORTIMER TO TAKE HER PLACE BY ELIZABETH'S SIDE TO SEARCH FOR SHAKESPEARE'S LOST PLAY. TO HER, THE PROFESSOR'S EXPERIENCE AND COURAGE, COMBINED WITH HER DAUGHTER'S SOLID KNOWLEDGE OF SHAKESPEARE'S WORKS, WILL MAKE THEM A FORMIDABLE TEAM.

Say no more, Sarah. How could I possibly abandon you and your charming daughter?

Drrriiiing

Oh? Are we expecting someone else?

That'll be Elizabeth. I was so sure of your support that I took the liberty of asking her to come. We don't have a second to lose.

I won't be of much further use here, Captain. I'll return to Venice on the morning train.

Of course, Salman. Have a good trip, and give the marquis my best!

A FEW MINUTES LATER...

Right, let's start by taking a look at that riddle that concludes the first part of Guglielmo da Spiri's autobiography.

I studied the text last night. Reading the last sentence...

...I believe I found the first lead to follow. Listen...

MEANWHILE, AT WANDSWORTH PRISON...

Listen to me, and try to get your neurons into gear. I won't have time to explain much more than the basics.

According to this text, the hunt for the documents will take place in several stages. I believe the first of those will be in Stratford-upon-Avon in Warwickshire. Which is where you'll be going this very morning...

29

IT'S PAST NINE O'CLOCK ON THE MORNING OF 30 AUGUST WHEN ELIZABETH MCKENZIE'S AUSTIN LEAVES OXFORD BEHIND TO CONTINUE NORTH-WEST.

I'd better stop for a while. Reading in a car doesn't agree with me.

We still have some time before arriving in Stratford. You should rest.

Actually, Professor, I know you a little better than you think...

How so, young lady?

PROFESSOR MORTIMER HAS TAKEN THE WHEEL WHILE THE YOUNG LADY REREADS GUGLIELMO DA SPIRI'S FIRST TEXT.

My mother told me about how you met in India, and the short romance that followed. As well as your recent reunion in Africa.*

Oh? Well... I... I hope that didn't make you ... uncomfortable?

Not at all! My mother remembers you as a perfect gentleman.

That's better! Your mother's esteem is very important to me, and I'd be honoured to gain yours, Elizabeth.

So would I, Professor. We'll have plenty of time to get to know each other better during our mission, and I'm delighted about it!

*SEE PART 1 OF THE SARCOPHAGI OF THE SIXTH CONTINENT AND THE GONDWANA SHRINE

Speaking of our mission, please would you reread the riddle Guglielmo left at the end of the first part of his story?

It says: 'Listen to me closely, my friends. I have observed the gaze of the effigy of Stratford's genius. And behind his pupils, deep inside his head, I have seen the first of three keys that will lead you to the last tragedy.'

My mother believes that the word 'effigy' could refer to Shakespeare's bust in Holy Trinity Church, where he is buried. That sculpture is the only recorded effigy from that time.

And so 'behind his pupils, deep inside his head' could mean literally 'inside the sculpture's head'. It makes sense...

32

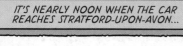

IT'S NEARLY NOON WHEN THE CAR REACHES STRATFORD-UPON-AVON...

This is the house where Shakespeare was born. I've visited it many times. There are no paintings of him at the time described in da Spiri's document...

...nor is there a portrait engraved on his tombstone — the one with the famous epitaph that has entranced so many mystery lovers.

I probably learnt it in school, but if you could refresh my memory...

Shakespeare himself had these words engraved: 'Good friend, for Jesus' sake forbear to dig the dust enclosed here; blessed be the man that spares these stones...'

'...and cursed be he that moves my bones.'

Yes, I remember now! Some claim that he had manuscripts buried with him and wanted to protect them.

Here we are.

Holy Trinity Church!

The tomb is at the back, in the chancel.

Oh! Good Lord!

Shakespeare's bust! That's it! His effigy... Someone's...

Shhh! Did you hear that?

It came from behind this door... Come on!

By Jove!

31

33

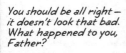

You should be all right — it doesn't look that bad. What happened to you, Father?

A couple of tourists came. They asked where Shakespeare's bust was, and then one of them aimed a revolver at me while the other climbed onto a chair to ... tip it onto the floor! Lord almighty! It's terrible...

The sculpture shattered, and they kept hammering at the head with a candlestick. Then those madmen took a close look at the pieces and swore angrily. When they heard you come in, they knocked me out. I just came to...

In other words, Salman's attackers got here first. They had the same idea we had, but came away empty-handed.

Which also brings us back to square one. The riddle alludes to an effigy that existed at the beginning of the 17th century. But we aren't aware of any other than this one...

Our only other clue is that mention of the Serenissima...

If it isn't in Stratford, then the answer to our riddle must be in Venice — I'm convinced of it. We have to go and inspect the palazzo of Marquis Da Spiri.

In Venice?! Aren't you forgetting that the air-traffic controllers' strike is still on ... and that time is of the essence?

If it's any help, there's a night train from London to Venice that leaves this evening. I know because my brother took it last week.

Excellent suggestion! If we call Blake so he'll book our tickets and then hurry, we can still make it.

Sorry, Father, but we have to leave you.

Don't worry about it. And if you get your hands on those Americans, send them to me for penance. I'd love to have a word with them!

Wait a minute — did you say Americans?! Like Salman's attackers ... who drove a 'big blue car' ... like the one I saw as we arrived...

Did you see him? That was Mortimer! Things just got more complicated. I need to talk to the boss.

We won't be back in time for a visit to Wandsworth.

Stop when you see a gas station. We'll give him a call.

AND 20 MINUTES LATER...

...On the contrary... The good professor is going to help you with your investigations. Follow him to Venice ... and while you're on the train, check whether he or his young partner have documents we don't know about.

WITHOUT ANOTHER WORD, MORTIMER SPRINTS OUT OF THE CHURCH ... JUST IN TIME TO SEE THE FORD DRIVE AWAY.

Blast! Too late!

THAT SAME EVENING IN LONDON, ON A PLATFORM AT VICTORIA STATION...

Still! We're wasting valuable time because of those strikes...

Look on the bright side. There were only a handful of tickets left, and you got two.

Remember that uncovering the historical truth is more important than the financial aspect of this whole case or staying within its attendant deadline. Enjoy your trip and the charming company in which I'm leaving you.

You're right, Sarah. But you know me. I can't help but wanting to beat our competitors to the punch —especially if they happen to be dishonest!

Don't worry... After all, the air-traffic controllers' strike applies to them too.

I propose that we take time to settle in and then meet in the dining carriage.

Very well. I'll bring da Spiri's document. We can go over it again and who knows, maybe we'll find new clues...

NIGHT HAS FALLEN BY THE TIME ELIZABETH AND THE PROFESSOR ARE TOGETHER AGAIN, READY TO TAKE STOCK OF THEIR SITUATION OVER A GOOD DINNER.

Now that we have time, could you translate Guglielmo da Spiri's text for me? I'd never be able to do it myself. I've quite forgotten what little Latin I learnt in my youth.

I'll be glad to, then...

'For the attention of future generations, here is the real story of the great Shake-Speares...

'My father, Marquis Alessandro da Spiri, was, along with his brother Giulio, heir to a rich family of Venetian merchants. As part of my education, he had sent me to England to stay with one of his friends, Sir Alexander Hoghton.

33

'This was where, in April 1580, I met William Shake. On the recommendation of his former schoolteacher in Stratford, William had just entered Sir Alexander's service as a schoolmaster and was staying at Hoghton Tower.

'Born on 23 April 1564, and a Catholic like me, he was the third child of Johannes Shake, a prosperous glover and alderman of Stratford, and Mary Arden, member of the local gentry.

'I was immediately won over by the charm of that silver-tongued young man. We soon became fast friends.

'I was fascinated by science and arts, whereas he loved only to sing and play the clown. Not that he didn't put a certain elegance into it, whether in gesture or words, for a rough provincial.

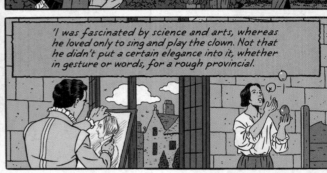

'Like me, he had just turned sixteen. Back then, and at first glance, that was the only thing we had in common...'

'...apart from both being passionately fond of the theatre. Like him, I would see stories unfold in my head that were far more enthralling than any we were given the chance to watch...

'Unfortunately, my position as a noble and heir to the family's business would not let me take these aspirations beyond mere dreams. I would find solace in telling William all the stories I'd heard during my trip across Europe, from my native Venetia to the Northern Kingdoms...

'From the old Italian legend of Romeus and Giulietta to the Germanic saga of King Horwendil, murdered by his brother Feng, I made my friend travel along the infinite roads of a culture he had never known.

Then he would reinvent these stories with his own characters and turns of phrase, until they became magical! And so would life go on at Hoghton Tower, happy and carefree...'

Waiter, please!

Do you realise, Professor?

Absolutely every detail mentioned by da Spiri corroborates the meagre information gathered by historians.

Fascinating, indeed! Do go on reading, please.

Then my father ordered me to return to Venice. It was with a heavy heart and the hope of quickly coming back to my dear poet that I boarded the ship.

'Five years later my father passed away. I inherited half the family fortune. When I proposed to Uncle Giulio that I should go and represent our business interests in London, I also inherited a new-found freedom.

'Imagine my surprise when, visiting Stratford the next spring, I discovered that the merry youth I remembered had become the glum husband of a certain Anne Hathaway — a distinctly insipid orphan eight years older than him!

'After his stay in Hoghton, William had found employment with a solicitor near Stratford. There he had indeed learnt to polish his skill at playing with words ... but also with hearts.

'William told me of his indiscretion and of how this Anne had entrapped him with the oldest weapon in the world. When I saw him again, his daughter Susanna was almost two already, and twins Hamnet and Judith had just been born. My friend was bored to tears in that life — that much was obvious.

'Another thing quickly became obvious: Anne Hathaway took a very dim view of my influence upon her husband who, at my side, appeared to find a new appetite for life...

'A short while later, the troupe of a certain Ferdinando Stanley came through Stratford, and William became completely entranced while watching the performance.

'I can still hear my friend: "It's settled, Guglielmo. I have but one life ... and it is in a theatre that it will find its true meaning! Tomorrow I'll be leaving with that troupe. London awaits... And if you so wish, London awaits us *both*!"

'And so, the next morning, William Shake left wife and children to go to London and perform King Leir, The Troublesome Reign of King John and other famous works that would largely inspire our own future plays.'

Do you see? This testimony finally explains how a young English provincial had access to all those foreign sources and culture!

What do you mean?

35

Most of Shakespeare's plays were inspired by ancient tales. There was nothing shocking about such borrowings back then. The times were still steeped in oral tradition. It wasn't called plagiarism — merely 'bringing back into fashion'.

The main question was always knowing how the son of a small provincial trader could have had access to all the culture necessary to write such a richly documented body of works.

This all seems to indicate that we're on the right track! Go on!

Here's the answer. It was thanks to his friend Guglielmo da Spiri!

I'd like nothing better, especially as we were about to address the infamous 'lost years' of Shakespeare's life!

Lost years?

Yes. We know absolutely nothing about the author's life from 1585 to 1592. By the time his name resurfaces, Shakespeare has become a successful actor and playwright. Unfortunately, the text stops here...

...Well... It stops with this last statement in the form of a riddle: 'Listen to me closely, my friends. I have observed the gaze of the effigy of Stratford's genius. And behind his pupils, deep inside his head, I have seen the first of three keys that will lead you to the last tragedy.'

Let's hope we'll find it in Venice... If you don't mind, I'm going to think this over in my cabin!

Let's not lose heart, young lady! Do try to get some sleep too. Venice will bring us more answers than Stratford — I'm sure of it.

AS OUR TWO TRAVELLERS RETURN TO THEIR CABINS FOR A FEW HOURS OF REST...

...STRANGE GOINGS-ON TAKE PLACE IN THE HALLWAY OF THEIR CARRIAGE.

Ow!

The coast is clear. Go ahead.

Room service, miss. I wanted to make sure you'd received your water.

My water?... But I never ord...

You'd better not scream...

Wait a minute, steward! What is...?

Ouch!

Don't try anything funny, girly. Just hand over all the documents about...

Yowch!

Elizabeth?! I...

You lout! I'm going to teach you some good manners!

Oof!

Hey! You! I...

?!

Pak!

Ow!

Elizabeth?!...

I'm sorry... I...   Yes, yes... Don't worry about me — go after him!

He's not going anywhere...

BUT LUCK SIMPLY ISN'T WITH THE PROFESSOR TONIGHT...

AFTER LOSING TRACK OF THE FUGITIVE, MORTIMER RETURNS TO HIS TRAVELLING COMPANION.

That scoundrel must have thought we had more information than he did. No documents for him — but a good karate lesson instead!

You're definitely full of surprises, young lady. Still, don't open your door for anybody until I come for you tomorrow morning.

Without the moustache, and with sunglasses on to hide the black eye, I doubt she'll recognise me.

Yeah... Well, no need to be overzealous! From now on, we just watch them and let them find the stuff for us.

37

WHILE THE NIGHT EXPRESS CONTINUES ON ITS WAY TO VENICE, BACK IN LONDON, ANOTHER ROBBERY IS ABOUT TO BE COMMITTED IN GROSVENOR SQUARE.

What is this?... Who are you? I'm going to call the...

Stow it, flunky. You're not going to call anyone.

By Saint George! Jasper, what is all this hullabaloo?!

That's him! Get him!

By Saint Gregory!

By Saint Augustine stay calm, Jude... Dial 999...

BAM!

BAM!

Police?! Help!

CRAACK!

DESPERATELY TRYING TO ESCAPE, MR BRIDGES MAKES A DASH FOR THE DOOR...

!

Dammit! Stop him!

Not so fast, mate!

Oww!

Bom!

Yikes!

D'you think he's dead? I don't want to be no murderer...

He's breathing. But we can't wait for him to wake up. Maybe the flunky knows the combination to the safe.

I doubt it. And if the solicitor had time to call the police, we'd better scarper! To hell with old Sandfield's will.

AROUND 1 A.M. THE POLICE HAVE ARRIVED, ALERTED BY MR BRIDGES AT THE LAST SECOND.

He was lucky. You were right not to move him until the ambulance arrived.

JASPER DESCRIBES THE ATTACKERS...

Keen sense of observation you have there, Jasper. You were probably dealing with one of those gangs of Teddy boys that have been plaguing London lately. I need to make a phone call.

...Goodness! And you have no idea what their motives were? Breaking into private property isn't normal behaviour for those Teds...

You're right, Captain. Perhaps the solicitor can give us more details when he comes to. In the meantime, he's just been sent to hospital.

This home invasion is decidedly unusual... And at Mr Bridges' of all places...It's high time I have a closer look at the known associates of everyone involved in this case.

THE NEXT MORNING, THE TRIP HAVING CONCLUDED WITHOUT ANY FURTHER INCIDENTS, THE PASSENGERS OF THE LONDON EXPRESS ARRIVE AT SANTA LUCIA STATION IN VENICE.

Miss! Professor!

Hello Salman.

Welcome to Venice! If you'd care to follow me.

What a lovely boat!

It's so shiny!

That'll be the twenty-four coats of varnish applied to Honduran mahogany that has been aged for ten years in the hangars of Sarnico. This is no mere boat, Miss McKenzie – this is a Riva*.

Avanti,** Roberto!

VROAAR

Dammit! We're going to lose them!

Easy, Freddy! Our hotel isn't far from the da Spiri palace. We'll find them again soon enough...

*LEGENDARY HIGH-END BOATBUILDERS IN SARNICO, NORTHERN ITALY.
**LET'S GO!

39

FOR THE YOUNG WOMAN, IN VENICE FOR THE FIRST TIME, IT'S A MAGICAL BOAT RIDE...

...THAT ENDS AT THE DOCK OF THE PALAZZO DA SPIRI...

...WHERE THE MARQUIS HAS COME TO GREET OUR FRIENDS.

Thank you for your welcome, Marquis.

Your visit is an honour for me, Professor Mortimer.

I imagine you'd like to see 'the cage' right away?

Indeed. Every second counts, as you know...

THE MASTER OF THE HOUSE LEADS HIS VISITORS TO THE SECRET CHAMBER, WHERE THE DISTURBING DUMMY AWAITS IN HIS GLASS PRISON.

It's ... fascinating!

It looks like the lock is linked to some sort of ... mechanism...

...A self-destruct mechanism, yes. Leonardo da Vinci had already created similar systems, and it is said he was a regular guest at the Palazzo da Spiri...

According to Marcello Lamberti, my watchmaker friend, the contraption is designed to ensure the destruction of the paper, should the lock be picked or broken.

My ancestor's letter mentioned three keys to be found. And yet there are only two keyholes.

Perhaps a single key will in fact fit both. We'll worry about that later. I think we can go back upstairs.

AFTER HALF AN HOUR OUR FRIENDS HAVE FINISHED RECOUNTING THE PROGRESS THEY'VE MADE IN THEIR INVESTIGATION.

We know of no authenticated portrait of the author made in his lifetime. But if the word 'effigy' means 'sculpture', we've already ascertained that the bust in Stratford wasn't it. So we thought that the solution must be here, in Venice...

You may be more right than you know, dear friends...

...as the answer is perhaps in this very room! In this library, whose sculptures were made by the hand of my ancestor Guglielmo!

These busts represent important figures of science or letters during Classical times. All but one, whose identity has long been a mystery. Now that you've made me think of it, though, it could indeed be...

He looks younger, but ... there's no doubt! This is the same face as the Stratford bust. Shakespeare!

May I?

By all means. Be careful, they're on the heavy side...

Indeed. It's not hollow. Nothing could be hiding inside that head — 'behind his pupils'.

Wait a minute! My ancestor had made copies of these sculptures. They lay forgotten in the cellars of the palazzo for centuries. A few years ago I donated them to my friend Peggy Newgold for her private museum.

Plaster copies?! Of course! Those are the ones we need to see!

Peggy is one of my most delightful friends. Salman will take you to her home. A prior commitment prevents me from going with you, but I'll call ahead to tell her you're coming.

HAVING THANKED THEIR HOST, MORTIMER AND ELIZABETH IMMEDIATELY BOARD THE RIVA AGAIN...

...WHILE THE MARQUIS CALLS HIS FRIEND.

...And according to the professor, the mystery of the glass cage could be partly unravelled at your place, thanks to one of your plaster busts!

This is all wonderfully exciting! Don't worry, dear. I'm going to meet them right away and show them that bust...

Ah! Dear absent-minded Stefano forgot to tell me something!

Driiiing! Drrriiiing!

Oh! It's you, Abigail, darling!... How are you? As it happens, things are speeding up here... Yes! Stefano is sending me some friends of his who are continuing the investigation. And you'll never guess where it's led them!...

Your place?! That is rather unexpected indeed!... Yes, of course... But only if you promise to keep me informed... I'm counting on you, my dear!... Yes! Arrivederci!*

I think I just called the right person ... at the right time. We must contact our man in Venice. Quickly!

MOMENTS LATER, IN A SMALL VENETIAN HOTEL A STONE'S THROW FROM THE PALAZZO DA SPIRI.

Hello? Yes, sir... OK... Yes, I wrote down the address. We're already on our way.

*GOODBYE!

41

43

MEANWHILE, ELIZABETH AND THE PROFESSOR HAVE ARRIVED AT THE HOME OF THE WELL-KNOWN ECCENTRIC BILLIONAIRE PEGGY NEWGOLD.

This plaster copy is rather light. Part of it could be hollow.

Could what we're looking for be hidden inside? How to be sure?

There's only one way to check!

It's just a copy, after all!

CRASH

A case! Let's go open it! The suspense is killing me!

That's it! The second part of Guglielmo da Spiri's story ... and a key!

Go ahead and read it, Elizabeth. Remember that we only have about 30 hours left.

'From 1585 on and for many years, life passed like a dream, albeit in extreme discretion. William performed in the greatest theatres of London and, when I wasn't travelling, I had my uncle send me money to cover both our rents...

'London was a city where everything was possible. In the anonymity of a crowd, we could live in harmony without anyone paying attention to our very different social backgrounds. But we still needed to be careful...

'...If my uncle ever learnt that I associated with an actor, our beautiful freedom would be well and truly over.

Rats! That black butler again! We'll have to go around the back...

'We had set up a hidden cache in the Globe Theatre's external foundations where we could leave our messages and arrange our meetings discreetly.

'It was around that time that we had this fabulous idea. The classical repertoire, devoid of humour or witty repartee, felt terribly boring to us...

'Together, we would write our own plays!'

...I'll bring you my knowledge of exotic tales and courtly games, and you, with your talent as a storyteller, will write texts that will move audiences to tears!

You read me like an open book, my Fair Lord!

'William wanted us to sign our work jointly, but it wasn't really feasible.

It would mean the end of my freedom, and I'd have to say goodbye to my uncle's money. But I do not care for fame, anyway. All that matters is that our plays meet with success!

'William stared at me for a long time, then declared that he would now call me his "Wistful Hero". And as "Guglielmo" was the translation of "William" and my name, da Spiri, couldn't appear publicly...

'...he decided to play with the words, so that the name William Shake-Speares would be etched on people's minds as the unique author of our joint work.

'And soon, after I commissioned some sonnets in order to pay him without injuring his pride, my dear friend not only dedicated them to me, his "Wistful Hero", but also signed the collection in our new name.

'Later, once his fortune allowed him to do so, William even went so far as to have his name modified on some official documents concerning him: he had my part of the name added. That way our works would go down in history without anyone being able to separate us.'

So there's the hidden truth. William Shakespeare was ... two people behind a single body of work! Incredible!

That also explains the strange spelling of his name on the collection of sonnets, and that dedication to the mysterious Mr W.H. It was meant for his 'Wistful Hero' — Guglielmo da Spiri!

What else does the text say? We have to solve the next riddle, quickly...

As we know, the Lost Years were rich in creations. In 1591 the great popular successes began: Henry VI, Richard III... And the following years were even more productive!

Between 1594 and 1596 came the plays Romeo and Juliet, A Midsummer Night's Dream and The Merchant of Venice... Then, in 1603, James I succeeded Elizabeth I and our two writers became court favourites.

There followed more masterpieces: Othello, King Lear, Macbeth, to name just the most famous ones!

Ah, but this is new... Listen to this, Professor!

43

'In 1608 I returned from a brief trip to Venice with Ornella, my Uncle Giulio's daughter that he had asked me to chaperone in London.

'She instantly captured William's heart, and just as quickly became his muse – the "Dark Lady" of his later sonnets...

'Ornella kept finding new excuses to avoid returning to Venice. And so, early in 1613, her father eventually sent a spy to London.

'When my uncle learnt that Ornella and I had a distinctly unconventional relationship with William, he ordered me to return to Venice forthwith with my cousin, on pain of cutting us off.

The threat also extended to our dear poet, whom the spy had described to the marquis as "a disreputable character and a bad influence".'

...I must add that should you refuse, your thespian 'friend' too will feel your uncle's wrath.

'Sick at heart, we obeyed the command without arguing. I had just enough time to leave a note in our hiding place at the Globe Theatre, which said the following...

'"29 June 1613. My dear W., for your safety as much as ours, Ornella and I are leaving for Venice this very night, alas. I am taking our latest play project to keep it safe...

'"...If you read these lines, leave us one last message in the coffer. I will try to come and take it before we depart. Take good care of yourself, dear friend, and rest assured that we shall come back! G."

'But when, that evening, I went to see if William had left an answer, I arrived to find the Globe Theatre ablaze! Fireworks had set the thatched roof on fire.

'We were thus forced to board the ship without knowing if our beloved friend had found our goodbyes.'

46

This confirms that William was in fact the author of the note found by the Thames flushermen in 1858. He did find the goodbye note on 29 June 1613 and left his answer in the hiding place as agreed.

The Globe Theatre did indeed burn to the ground that evening, and the metal coffer holding the answer disappeared in the muddy waters of the Thames … until its miraculous reappearance in 1858 during the Great Stink.

That's right! The author of the note expressed his hope of seeing his friends again some day – it was obviously William's answer to Guglielmo and Ornella! Go on!

'Two years went by with no news from William. As I'd got back to sculpting, I tried to carve his face from memory.

'But in early 1616, Ornella's father's in turn passed away. This time we were free from the supervision of our family once and for all. We immediately set sail for London…

'…where we learnt that our friend had left the theatre.

'One rumour claimed that he had returned to Stratford. Another that he was letting himself die of boredom there. We didn't even take the time to rest.

'In the house he had purchased, New Place, we found our friend lying in bed. When he saw us, a smile came to him that seemed to erase all his pains. He asked his wife to leave us alone…'

And the text ends with this strange sentence – which is probably another riddle…

Quick! Tell us!

The truth about a playwright cannot be told but on set. And what finer set than that of the ancient theatre resurrected for the cursed lovers? Friends, the key to success is to humbly kneel before the glorious arches. Between the two long stones, not even the slimmest finger shall pass.'

Let's see… What could be the 'ancient theatre resurrected for the cursed lovers'?

For a start, knowing who those 'cursed lovers' are would help…

45

There's a plethora of lovers in Shakespeare's works!

Yes, of course! The lovers of Verona! And what is it you can find in Verona?

I read that you can visit the supposed houses of Capulet and Montaigu... But no one knows if those places existed in Shakespeare's time.

I'm not talking about those tourist traps, but about the famous arena — the Roman amphitheatre. Destroyed by an earthquake in the 12th century ... it was restored during the Renaissance!

Perhaps, but two of them remain far better known than any others... Romeo and Juliet!

Hence the line: 'the ancient theatre resurrected'. By Jove! You're right!

And if the 'key to success' refers to one of the three keys mentioned in the first message ... it works!

As for the glorious arches of the riddle, you can't miss them — they make up the entire structure. You'll have to find out which ones are meant.

There isn't a moment to lose. What's the quickest way to get to Verona?

Not so fast!

Nice to see you again, old buddy!

I don't believe we've been introduced, but the way you came bursting in suggests you have never been taught proper manners.

I see you're still as good at making big speeches as you are at solving riddles, Professor!

Sharkey*!?

*SEE THE MYSTERY OF THE GREAT PYRAMID AND SOS METEORS

You recognise me. I'm touched... I'd especially like to thank you for your brilliant deductions — they're going to save me a lot of time. Now if you wouldn't mind turning around...

I need a few hours' head start on you.

Ow!

I hope you'll forgive us if we don't stay for tea, ladies. We have some urgent business to deal with.

SHARKEY AND FREDDY IMMEDIATELY RETURN TO THE DOCK, WHERE A WATER TAXI AWAITS THEM.

Start the engine, driver! Take us somewhere we can rent a car.

He's coming to!

Thank God! I was so scared that brute had...

How are you feeling?

A couple of aspirins should do the trick.

I'll go get you some.

Not only did we give those gangsters the answer to the second riddle, but we also gave them several hours' head start!

Whether those villains decided to drive to Verona or take the next train, I can help you catch up with them.... Salman will take you to my garage.

I suggest the first car on the left when you go in. With that one, you'll be in Verona before anyone else!

Thank you for everything, Mrs Newgold. One last thing: did you tell anyone about us visiting you?

Me? But I only got word that you were coming just before...

Holy cow! My friend, Countess Abigail of Chatham, called me to see how I was doing, and... Yes, I did. I told her you were coming. Surely you don't think that she could have warned those...?

Call Captain Francis Blake at MI5 in London. Tell him what happened and ask him to investigate that Countess of Chatham.

You can count on me, Professor. And be careful, my friends!

NOT LONG AFTER, THE RIVA REACHES ITS DESTINATION NEAR LIBERTY BRIDGE...

WASTING NO TIME, SALMAN TAKES OUR FRIENDS TO THE DOOR OF A VAST HANGAR...

...WHERE THEY DISCOVER ANOTHER SIDE OF PEGGY NEWGOLD'S COLLECTIONS.

47

49

WHILE MORTIMER AND ELIZABETH ROAR TOWARDS VERONA IN THEIR POWERFUL FERRARI TESTAROSSA...

...IN LONDON, FRANCIS BLAKE HAS JUST BEEN ON THE PHONE TO PEGGY NEWGOLD.

A problem, Captain?

That was a friend of Professor Mortimer's. She gave me a very strange testimony.

David, could you discreetly look into the Countess Abigail of Chatham? I'd like to know who the real person is behind the Count's wife...

Also, do you have the copy of Lord Lupus Sandfield's will and the report on his descendants I asked you for?

Here they are, Captain.

HAVING SWALLOWED UP THE 80 MILES BETWEEN VENICE AND VERONA IN RECORD TIME, OUR FRIENDS HAVE ENTERED THE ANCIENT CITY.

ON THAT 31 AUGUST, THE YEARLY OPERA FESTIVAL DRAWS A DENSE CROWD TO THE FAMOUS ARENA.

Wit-woo! Ciao, bella*! I'd love to take you out for a spin!

A gentleman doesn't speak to a lady that way, young man. He introduces himself, for starters!

Oh! Mi scusi, signore*... My name is Luigi.

*HELLO, BEAUTIFUL!   *I'M SORRY, SIR...

I wasn't addressing the young lady, Signore, but ... your magnificent Ferrari.

Ha! Ha! Ha! I'm not entirely certain that makes it better, but at least it's funny. No doubt about it — we're in Italy!

I suppose I was a bit abrupt... By way of apology, I'll buy all your letter openers if you show us a quicker way to the arena.

It's a deal, Signore!

AND, TEN MINUTES OF INVALUABLE SHORTCUTS LATER...

Remember Guglielmo's words: '... Friends, the key to success is to humbly kneel before the glorious arches. Between the two long stones, not even the slimmest finger shall pass.'

The two 'long stones'... There!

Let's see if that young man's letter opener will do the trick...

The mortar is old and hardened. It's crumbling... There's an empty space behind... Yes... I can feel something!

SOON AFTERWARDS, IT'S SHARKEY AND FREDDY'S TURN TO ARRIVE AT VERONA'S ARENA...

Hey!

Beebeeep! Beebeeep!

According to what the boss told me, it should be that way.

The two long stones!... Darn it! That's impossible! How could they have...?

'Sorry, Mr Sharkey. This riddle was not meant to be solved by uneducated henchmen. I'll see you again .... in London! Philip Mortimer'...

Gaah!

MEANWHILE, THE FERRARI IS NOW SWALLOWING THE MILES BETWEEN VERONA AND VENICE IN THE OPPOSITE DIRECTION.

I'll admit that leaving that note was rather childish of me, but picturing Sharkey's face reading it is such a pleasure!

And here's the second key... This one's made of silver!

We don't have much time to find the third. In the meanwhile, why don't you read out the rest of Guglielmo da Spiri's manuscript?

All right. But promise me you'll stop me if you get tired.

You morons!... I really can't count on anyone but myself! Well... At least the radio just announced the end of the strike at London's airports.

If they find that document, they'll come back tomorrow. Get back to London and keep your eye on flights coming from Venice until 5 p.m. After that it won't matter any more.

49

51

Where were we? Oh yes! Guglielmo and Ornella had just discovered a dying William, lying in his bed in Stratford...

'Upon seeing us, as if by a miracle, William's condition appeared to improve. Life came back to his eyes. At that moment, another of his friends arrived — one whom I recognised immediately: Ben Jonson!'

Ben Jonson? The other major playwright of the time?

Nothing surprising there. According to specialists, the admiration and friendship between Shakespeare and Jonson was quite genuine.

ENTHRALLED BY THE CONVERSATION, MORTIMER SEEMS TO FORGET THAT IN ITALY...

...CARS DRIVE ON THE RIGHT!

Pwwwon!

Look out!

EEEEEEEE

SCRRRSSSSSH

Ooof! Another four inches and...

Phew!

You're absolutely exhausted, Professor, and it's almost night. Since fate drove us to this hotel, let's make the most of it and rest here. If we were to be reckless, even for Shakespeare's sake, my mother would never forgive us!

You are wiser than I am, young lady, and you're right. A good meal and a few hours' sleep will do us a world of good.

52

AFTER FRESHENING UP, MORTIMER AND ELIZABETH HAVE ENJOYED A DELICIOUS *BIGOI CO' L'ARNA** SERVED WITH A SUPERB BOTTLE OF BARDOLINO SUPERIORE.

Are you ready Professor? Here's the rest of it...

'William then explained his idea to us — an idea worthy of one of our plays! He no longer wanted to let himself die. On the contrary! He wanted to end his life a free man, with us ... and in Venice!

'With the complicity of Jonson, whom he thanked by giving him the publishing rights to our texts, William devised a rather simple plan. He was going to order his family to leave him to face death alone.

*VENETIAN FORM OF *BIGOLI CON L'ANATRA* — WHOLEWHEAT PASTA WITH DUCK SAUCE.

'William would ask his wife to leave the task of burying him to his friend Ben, so that his family would remember him as a lively and smiling man.

'At night, Ben Jonson would bring in the corpse of a vagrant that he'd buy from the guardian of a pauper's grave. He'd wrap it in a shroud and place it inside the coffin intended for William — who would flee the house that same night...

'...after writing the short epitaph he wanted to see carved on the tomb he'd already paid for in the village church.

The text was meant to be sufficiently scary to dissuade anyone from ever opening the grave — even those who might one day want to bury his wife with him. With time, anyway, no one would be able to identify the body...

'And so it happened!... While his family and friends believed they were burying him in Stratford...

'...William was waiting for us to set sail for Venice once and for all...'

Are you serious? Shakespeare didn't die in May 1616? And he isn't buried in Stratford?!

Not according to this account, at least... Listen to the rest...

51

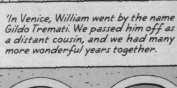

'In Venice, William went by the name Gildo Tremati. We passed him off as a distant cousin, and we had many more wonderful years together.

'In 1623, a captain of the da Spiri merchant fleet brought back a collected works of Shakespeare that had just been published in London by Heminge and Condell.

'When we opened it, we discovered the dedication by dear Ben Jonson. It was a message to us; a simple phrase we alone could understand...

'Thou art a monument without a tomb, and art alive still while thy book doth live.'

That's it... Ben Jonson's dedication in the 1623 First Folio! No one knew how the publishers had managed to obtain Shakespeare's plays, eighteen of which had never been printed. Now it makes sense!

I'm impressed by the depth of your knowledge, Elizabeth! What then?

'The years went by, happy and peaceful... Alas, my cousin Ornella was the first to leave us in February 1630. The death of his Dark Lady cast William into the depths of despair. His health began to deteriorate and he seemed to lose any will to fight.

'A few months later, William passed away too. Keeping the promise that I'd made him, I secretly had his remains laid next to Ornella's.

Two more years went by. With a small group of friends of quality, we created a brotherhood that organised intellectual jousts.

'But I was growing weary of life in soul and body. In private I set to work so that I could die while keeping my word... I had a clockwork mechanism to put together.

'Now, in this summer of 1632, it is time for me to leave this world. I shall entrust my life to sweet Cantarella and the truth of the works of Shake-Speares to whichever of my friends knows how to find it.

Tonight, dear friends and members of the brotherhood, I have invited you to dinner. My faithful Dino will ensure that you have everything you desire. Please forgive my absence from the table...

'...and I hope that the wisest among you will preserve the memory of the great William Shakespeare! May he succeed in putting his last play into words so that, along with the rest of his works, it will delight theatres of the world for all time!'

These pages corroborate the testimony that the marquis read to us yesterday—most likely the faithful Dino's. Do you remember?

Yes. The dinner invitation for an evening in August 1632. The absence of the host. The small earthquake that drove the guests away...

The mechanism got stuck. Guglielmo's guests were never able to play his planned game or investigate...

...and the truth remained buried until the ship's collision restarted the mechanism that made the bell ring.

We still have to find the third key. There should be another riddle at the end of the text, shouldn't there?

Indeed there is...

To whoever reads these lines and will be daring enough to brave the dark eye that protects the reunited lovers: know that the last key of knowledge awaits at the gates of Hell, in the last capital of a bygone world!'

What does this mean?

Let's see... The reunited lovers' must be William and Ornella. If I heard you correctly, Guglielmo secretly had William entombed alongside his beloved...

Ornella da Spiri! Where could she have been buried ... if not in the family vault of such an ancient and noble line?!

Logical, my dear! We need to call the marquis!

A FEW MINUTES LATER...

The marquis just confirmed that since the 14th century, the da Spiri have had a family vault in the Basilica of San Francesco in ... Ravenna.

Ravenna! The last capital of the Roman Empire! In other words ... 'a bygone world'!

...And according to the marquis, it's also where Dante is buried—author of ...the Inferno!* It all fits! We have to go to Ravenna!

I must confess I'm exhausted. It's a fairly long drive to Ravenna... Let's get a few hours' sleep, as we have practically no hope left of bringing proof back to London in time.

All right. But we leave for Ravenna at dawn. You never know what helpful nudge fate might send our way.

I admire your unwavering optimism. Just as I understand the fondness and admiration that my mother has for you!

Your culture and intelligence are matched only by your kindness, Elizabeth. Sleep well.

Goodnight, Professor.

*HELL – FIRST PART OF THE EPIC POEM DIVINE COMEDY (1320) BY ITALIAN POET DANTE ALIGHIERI.

53

THE NEXT DAY. IT ISN'T QUITE 8 A.M. BY THE TIME THE POWERFUL FERRARI ENTERS RAVENNA.

?!

Professor, stop! Look at that!

There on the newspaper! The air-traffic controllers' strike is over!

Daily Mirror
END OF STRIKE IN BRITISH AIRPORTS

There's your nudge from fate, I believe! We still have a small chance of getting the evidence back in time!

A FEW MINUTES LATER, THE CAR HAS STOPPED IN FRONT OF THE BASILICA OF SAN FRANCESCO.

It's this way.

Here we are!

I feel moved... Can you imagine? William Shakespeare and Ornella da Spiri, his Dark Lady, have been sleeping side by side here for three and a half centuries...

ORNELLA DA SPIRI

...And this should be the 'dark eye that protects the reunited lovers'.

CLICK

Look. It looks like a tiny space ... just large enough for...

CRRRR

...this lead key ... and this folded piece of paper. Quick! Translate it!

G

'One choice remains for you to make, friend of Shakespeare's work, for only one of these three keys leads to the ultimate play. And none, if you choose wrong... The answer lies both within the Serenissima and the playwright's writings.'

We can be in Venice around ten. Let's not waste a minute and book tickets on the first flight to London right away!

56

AFTER TWO MORE HOURS ON THE ROAD, MORTIMER AND ELIZABETH HAVE GONE BACK TO THE ENTRANCE TO VENICE, WHERE SALMAN HAS BEEN WAITING TO TAKE THEM TO THE PALAZZO DA SPIRI...

...WHERE THEY RETURN TO THE SECRET CHAMBER WITH THE MASTER OF THE HOUSE.

Well! We're now facing the last problem: choosing the right key. The one that will disarm the destructive mechanism...

...assuming the contents of that phial are still active after more than three centuries...

Let's not take any chances.

We had time to ponder the last riddle during the drive back. And if the answer to it 'lies both within the Serenissima and the playwright's writings', we thought that...

Of course! For a 'friend of Shakespeare's work', the most emblematic play 'within the Serenissima' is without a doubt The Merchant of Venice.

Exactly! And remember the plot. In order to win Portia's hand in marriage, as per the terms of her father's will, Bassanio must choose between the gold, silver and lead caskets. What if the three keys of your ancestor's riddle are likened to the three caskets...?

Then you would choose ... the lead key of course!

Will you do the honours, Marquis? After all, these documents belong to you.

CLICK

It's working. And now the other lock.

First, let's remove this...

DESPITE ALL THE CARE THE MARQUIS PUTS INTO REMOVING THE GLASS TUBE, THE DUMMY'S HAND COMES OFF ... REVEALING HUMAN BONES.

Santo cielo!*

55

*GOOD HEAVENS!

This... This isn't a dummy...

...it's my ancestor... Guglielmo da Spiri!

So this is how he disappeared. Thanks to his clever mechanism, he walled himself in, then locked himself inside this cage, strapped himself to the chair ... and took poison.

That's right. When he speaks of 'sweet Cantarella' in his text, he's not alluding to a woman, but...

...to a poison by the same name. By the end of the 15th century, the use of deadly poisons, especially cantarella, had become a sort of art in Venice...

But ... don't you think that your ancestor, a Catholic, would have wanted to be buried with his family?

Of course he would. Don't forget that if it hadn't been for that earthquake, his friends would have found his body on that evening of 1632, and could have given him a proper Christian burial ... which I will do promptly myself.

So, Elizabeth? Are these pages the evidence that we were hoping for?

More or less...

It does appear to be the outline of an unpublished play in three acts, called Love and Other Ambitions and written in Elizabethan English. But it's only signed with an intertwined G and W. I don't know if that will constitute sufficient proof with regard to Lupus Sandfield's will...

One thing at a time – the most urgent being to return to London immediately! We only have six hours left. I'll call Blake so he can organise our travel.

I'll take you to the airport with Salman. Avanti!

MEANWHILE, IN LONDON...

...OUR FRIENDS ARE EAGERLY EXPECTED.

OK, I just checked. The next flight will be landing in two hours. It's the last one they can take if they want to have a chance of making it to the lawyer's on time. We've got time to wet our whistles.

Good idea!

AND AT THE SAME TIME AT MI5...

Well, gentlemen, since everyone knows what they have to do, all that's left is for me to wish you good luck!

58

IT'S ALMOST 4 P.M. WHEN THE FLIGHT FROM VENICE LANDS IN LONDON.

Dammit! They did it!...

Miss, sir... Anything special to declare?

Nothing special.

DAVID HONEYCHURCH, WHOM MORTIMER HAS RECOGNISED, DISCREETLY REACHES FOR A BLACK BRIEFCASE THAT IS IDENTICAL TO THE PROFESSOR'S.

Excellent. In that case, welcome to the United Kingdom.

MI5's cab is waiting for you outside as agreed. The driver is wearing a grey cap. Good luck, Professor.

I think that's the one...

Yes, sir, I see them.

Let's go.

I'll bet you anything that our shadows will make their move after the tunnel!

What did I tell you?!

Ha ha! It looks like you lost the game to an 'uneducated henchman', Professor. Still, you're kinda lucky. I wasn't ordered to get rid of you today.

Delighted to hear it, Mr Sharkey. I suppose this is what you want?...

57

Panel 1:

SHARKEY GETS BACK IN THE FORD, WHICH HURTLES OFF.

My colleagues will follow them discreetly. In the meantime, I'm taking you to the hospital where Mr Bridges, the solicitor, is waiting for you. Honeychurch should have already brought him the original documents.

Hello, Captain?...

...Kendall here... Yes, everything is going as planned...

...Yes. You were right... They must be very excited about their success because they've thrown all caution to the wind. They just stopped right in front of the Oxford Lodge...

Be careful, Kendall, and wait for reinforcements before moving in. I've dealt with those ruffians enough to know that they will stop at nothing.

Right, I must leave you. We've arrived at Lord Sandfield's. It's time to put our other bird in his cage...

MEANWHILE, MORTIMER AND ELIZABETH HAVE REACHED THE HOSPITAL WHERE JUDE BRIDGES IS BEING TREATED — UNDER SPECIAL POLICE PROTECTION.

Wait for me, Professor! We're here now!

We only have a few minutes left. I don't want to take any more chances!

Mr Bridges! At last!

Ah! I see that David's given you the original documents. Have you had time to read them?

Well, sir? Are the documents admissible? We're still on time, aren't we?

Don't worry, miss. I'm acknowledging that the documents were indeed handed to me before the deadline. That said, I still have to check whether they can be considered indisputable proof before I can proceed with executing Lord Sandfield's will.

I just spoke to Inspector Kendall, Lord Sandfield. The thieves acted as expected. They completely missed the switching of briefcases at the airport, where my deputy was playing customs officer...

As we speak, they are surrounded by the police. There is little doubt that the theft was ordered by Sir Walter of Oxford.

Our investigation of Countess Abigail of Chatham revealed that she was born Abigail De Vere. An authentic, though penniless, descendant of the original Earls of Oxford...

...and a prominent member of the Oxford Lodge, bastion of the anti-Stratfordians. It was she who informed Sir Walter of this entire business, and it was the latter who hired the bandits to retrieve the documents. You can rest assured that we will obtain their confessions.

The original documents should currently be in the hands of Mr Bridges the solicitor, who's still under close protection at the hospital... They'll have arrived in the nick of time, thus respecting the conditions of Lord Lupus Sandfield's will. I wanted to let you know in person.

Very good, Captain. What must happen will happen.

And now I'll bid you farewell, Lord Sandfield. Don't get up; I know the way out.

Thank you again for informing me yourself, Captain. Goodbye.

Sorry, but I'm not leaving ...and I'm going to explain why...

CLAP

Eeeeekkkr...

?

Evening, Father!...

Oscar?! What...? Where did you come from?

59

The old servants' passageways are still quite handy for observing your visitors and listening to your conversations...

Who is that fellow? What's he doing with that walking stick? So it was you who kept plundering the family's cane collection?

This fellow has turned out to be very useful for handling certain tasks unworthy of our rank. Relieving your gentry friends of their belongings, for example...

After all, it's not my fault if you and your father allowed the family fortune to go up in smoke, is it?

How dare you!? My father wasn't responsible for the wars that...

Don't bother. I'm going to have to curtail this conversation...

...and let Dickie break in through the window...

KLING

...before accidentally killing you during a burglary gone wrong. We have less than ten minutes left...

Kill me?! But... You're even more insane than I thought!

Insane? Not in the least, dear Father. Rather, it's you who have lost all reason — sacrificing this family's future to a century-old testament, to a stupid question of honour.

...Oh yes. I know everything. Including the fact that said testament is **only** valid if the documents make it to that solicitor Bridges before the deadline ... and also on condition that the last living heir to that fool Lupus Sandfield agrees to maintain the bequest!

Well, I signed that document! Your plan has failed, Oscar!

Wrong, Father!...

...In a minute you'll be dead. In the eyes of the law, I will immediately become the last heir... And it's not yet five o'clock, and I didn't sign anything, and that money will be legally mine!

By Saint George! You're my son, Oscar! Surely you're not going to...

Hurry up, Dickie. This is getting tiresome...

Aaah!

BANG

Forgive my fake exit earlier, Lord Sandfield. But it was in your interest, as I'm sure you'll agree.

Hunnnh!...

THAT SAME EVENING, SEVERAL NEWLY ACCUSED CRIMINALS ARRIVE AT WANDSWORTH PRISON TO AWAIT THEIR TRIALS...

...CAUSING QUITE A STIR AMONG THE INMATES.

...by the devil! Who's going to pay me?! And who's going to help me escape?!

What?! Sharkey, Freddy and ... Sir Walter?! Here?... But then...

Sorry, boss...

TWO DAYS LATER. IT'S TEATIME AT SARAH SUMMERTOWN'S.

...Having discovered that Lord Sandfield happened to live in the very street where that Teddy boy I chased all through Hyde Park simply vanished the other night, I surmised that there was an interesting coincidence there.

I remembered that Mr Bridges had commented on Lord Sandfield's son being 'difficult to handle', and decided to place the house under discreet surveillance.

That's how my men discovered that young Oscar Sandfield was nothing but a gang boss. He spied on his father and the gentry friends that would visit him...

...in order to give his Teds tips on what meetings those rich and ageing men — in other words, easy targets — were holding around Hyde Park, the hunting grounds of those rogues.

Rereading Lupus Sandfield's will, I realised that once Oscar learnt of the cancellation clause, he'd have no choice, if he wanted to keep his inheritance ... but to eliminate his father.

All I had to do was 'accidentally' let him know while informing his father, then wait for him to make his move...

While Sharkey and Freddy were leading Kendall straight to Sir Walter of Oxford with what they thought were the precious documents. Brilliant!

Thanks to you and your police counterparts, Captain, all of those villains were unmasked and caught in a single operation! That's impressive!

And thanks to you, Professor, we saved Shakespeare's last play!

'Saved' might be a bit of an exaggeration...

61

Don't forget that the document we found in the shrivelled hands of Guglielmo da Spiri only bears the initials W and G as a signature. It was therefore judged non-admissible by Mr Bridges, according to the terms of Lord Lupus Sandfield's will.

It was merely a synopsis of the last story written by William and Guglielmo, Love and Other Ambitions. The text was waiting to be fleshed out 'in Shakespeare fashion'. But the fact remains that the 'literary testament of the two William S.' is quite real.

Elizabeth is right to underline the importance of your discovery. Who cares about the money? Knowing the truth about the dual origin of Shakespeare's works is an immense satisfaction in itself.

Besides, as a perfect gentleman and man of honour, Lord Sandfield insisted on donating part of the money he's just recovered to the William Shakespeare Defenders' Society.

I forgot to mention: the marquis told us that the 'acid phial' was in fact filled with nothing but water, and that any of the three keys could have opened the door of the cage. The supposed destruction mechanism was nothing but an illusion intended to spice up Guglielmo da Spiri's treasure hunt and stimulate his friends' cogitative skills.

All's well that ends well, then. As we're still missing definitive proof, the only question that will remain in the public's mind will be ... 'to be or not to be ... Shakespeare?'

OUR TWO FRIENDS HAVE TAKEN THEIR LEAVE OF THEIR HOSTS.

I hope you're not too disappointed, Mother?

Absolutely not, my Lizzie.

We've unearthed an unparalleled historical truth. It doesn't matter if it's not made public knowledge. Mostly, I'm delighted that this whole adventure gave you a chance to meet my old friend Philip.

He's a wonderful man. I understand why you're so fond of him.

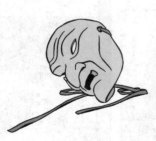

It's such a pity that Father never met him. I'm sure they would have got along famously.

You're right, my dear. I'm sure too.

THE END

Yves Sente
Juillard
Madeleine de Mille

64

THE ADVENTURES OF BLAKE & MORTIMER

1-The Yellow "M"
EDGAR P. JACOBS

2-The Mystery of the Great Pyramid Part 1
EDGAR P. JACOBS

3-The Mystery of the Great Pyramid Part 2
EDGAR P. JACOBS

4-The Francis Blake Affair
VAN HAMME - BENOIT

5-The Strange Encounter
VAN HAMME - BENOIT

6-S.O.S. Meteors
EDGAR P. JACOBS

7-The Affair of the Necklace
EDGAR P. JACOBS

8-The Voronov Plot
SENTE - JUILLARD

9-The Sarcophagi of the Sixth Continent Part 1
SENTE - JUILLARD

10-The Sarcophagi of the Sixth Continent Part 2
SENTE - JUILLARD

  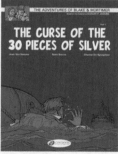  

11-The Gondwana Shrine
SENTE - JUILLARD

12-Atlantis Mystery
EDGAR P. JACOBS

13-The Curse of the 30 Pieces of Silver Part 1
VAN HAMME - STERNE - DE SPIEGELEER

14-The Curse of the 30 Pieces of Silver Part 2
VAN HAMME - AUBIN - SCHRÉDER

15-The Secret of the Swordfish Part 1
EDGAR P. JACOBS

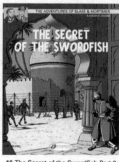    

16-The Secret of the Swordfish Part 2
EDGAR P. JACOBS

17-The Secret of the Swordfish Part 3
EDGAR P. JACOBS

18-The Oath of the Five Lords
SENTE - JUILLARD

19-The Time Trap
EDGAR P. JACOBS

20-The Septimus Wave
DUFAUX - AUBIN - SCHRÉDER

20-Plutarch's Staff
SENTE - JUILLARD

22-Professor Satō's Three Formulae Part 1
EDGAR P. JACOBS

23-Professor Satō's Three Formulae Part 2
JACOBS - DE MOOR

24-The Testament of William S.
SENTE - JUILLARD

THE OATH OF THE FIVE LORDS

Yves Sente   **André Juillard**

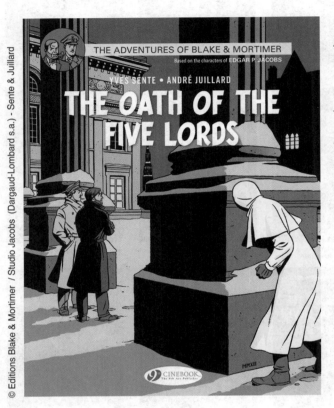

Based on the characters of EDGAR P. JACOBS

1919. Colonel Lawrence — Lawrence of Arabia — has an unpleasant meeting with an MI5 agent who confiscates his manuscript of *The Seven Pillars of Wisdom*. 35 years later, Oxford is shocked by a series of burglaries at the Ashmolean Museum, at the same time as Blake learns of the death of an old friend. The captain begins an investigation, while Mortimer looks into the thefts... But what dark connection does all of this have with Lawrence and Blake's own past?

André Juillard is a celebrated artist with a career spanning more than 35 years. He has worked on famous series such as "Les Sept Vies de L'Epervier" and "Masquerouge." In 1996, he was awarded the Grand Prix at the Angoulême festival.

Yves Sente began writing scripts in 1999. He has already acquired considerable clout, being chosen as successor to **Jean Van Hamme** for the series "Thorgal" (with **Grzegorz Rosinski**) and "XIII" (with **Iouri Jigounov**), and working with **Jean Van Hamme** on "Blake & Mortimer."

HAVING RUN TO THE FRONT DESK, THE CAPTAIN REQUESTS A CALL BE PLACED TO THE NUMBER PROFESSOR MORTIMER GAVE HIM...

Ah, it's ringing. I'll pass it on to you...

Philip, listen to me... I don't have time to explain anything at the moment. Just one thing: most likely there'll be other thefts at the Ashmolean, but I don't know what items will be targeted. Make sure surveillance is increased at the museum until I arrive. I'll call you back as soon as I can. See you soon!

I don't want to impose on you, miss, but could you place another call for me? It's a matter of life and death!

A MINUTE LATER, THE PHONE RINGS IN THE BUTLER'S OFFICE OF LORD RATHMORE'S RESIDENCE, AT THE HEIGHTS OF HIGH WYCOMBE.

Driiiiing! Driiiiing!

I'm sorry, sir. His Lordship is out... Sorry, sir, but I'm not authorised to tell you... I beg your pardon?!...

For the last time, for heaven's sake! I'm Captain Blake of MI5. This is an official call. It's a question of life and death for Lord Rathmore. I must know where he is — and quickly!

Ahem... In that case... His Lordship joined Lord Devlin for a spot of hunting... Yes... in the woods between their estates... What was that? Their old dispute? Hmm... After Lord Pickwick's funeral, I was led to believe that my master realised we all travel closer to the day when it becomes too late to work out our differences...

I beg you, try to make Lord Rathmore come back to the house. With or without Lord Devlin. But don't leave him alone until I get there, do you understand?... Perfect... I'm counting on you.

Hop in, David! I'll give you a rough outline of the case during the half-hour you have to get us to High Wycombe!

IMMEDIATELY, THE CAPTAIN'S DEPUTY LAUNCHES HIS VEHICLE ON THE 20 MILES OF SNOW-COVERED ROADS THAT WILL TAKE THEM TO THE OTHER SIDE OF THE CHILTERN HILLS.

21

THE OATH OF THE FIVE LORDS

PLUTARCH'S STAFF

Yves Sente **André Juillard**

Based on the characters of **EDGAR P. JACOBS**

BLAKE AND MORTIMER MUST HELP END A WAR ... TO PREPARE FOR THE NEXT ONE. OUR TWO HEROES' FIRST MISSION TOGETHER.

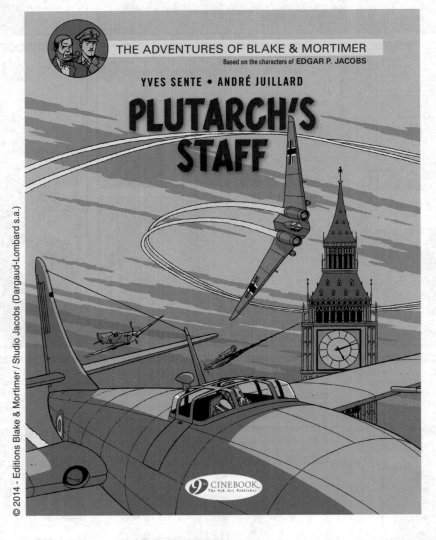

1944. England is still locked in a struggle to the death with Nazi Germany. But already a new threat looms among the peaks of the Himalayas. For now, though, Squadron Leader Blake, having saved London from a German prototype, is assigned to a top secret mission, during which he meets with an old friend he hasn't seen since India: Philip Mortimer. Soon, the pair are introduced to an officer working for Allied Intelligence: Colonel Olrik...

IN THIS SPRING OF 1944, THE PERMANENT HIGH-ALERT STATUS ON BOARD THE BRITISH AIRCRAFT CARRIER *INTREPID* IS A CONSTANT REMINDER TO THE ROYAL NAVY'S SAILORS AND PILOTS THAT A MERCILESS WAR IS STILL ENGULFING THE WORLD.

ON THE BRIDGE, CAPTAIN HAMILTON IS RECEIVING THE LATEST MISSION REPORT FROM SQUADRON LEADER FRANCIS BLAKE, RAF.

Three submarines sunk! You and your fellows have done great work, Blake!

The men are particularly earnest, Captain. The imminent prospect of an Allied landing in France has seen to that!

Unfortunately, the Germans are expecting it too. The alarming concentration of U-boats off our coasts confirms it.

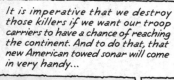

It is imperative that we destroy those killers if we want our troop carriers to have a chance of reaching the continent. And to do that, that new American towed sonar will come in very handy...

An American sonar?

It's top secret. Our allies have come up with a very low-frequency sound detector of previously unthinkable sensitivity. It should help us better detect underwater targets whose coordinates we can then forward to your fighter-bombers.

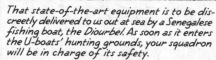

That state-of-the-art equipment is to be discreetly delivered to us out at sea by a Senegalese fishing boat, the *Diourbel*. As soon as it enters the U-boats' hunting grounds, your squadron will be in charge of its safety.

Captain! Urgent message from the Cabinet War Rooms!

1

PLUTARCH'S STAFF

Based on the characters of EDGAR P. JACOBS

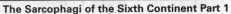

The Sarcophagi of the Sixth Continent Part 1

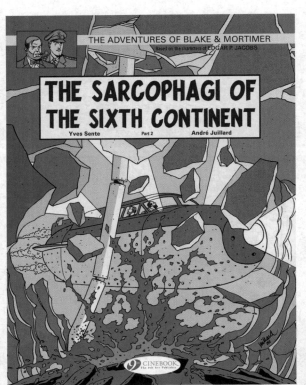

The Sarcophagi of the Sixth Continent Part 2

PROFESSOR MORTIMER'S PAST IN INDIA IS ABOUT TO CATCH UP WITH HIM... IN ANTARCTICA!

Philip Mortimer spent his youth in the land of the Maharajas. He loves India, but his last visit there did not end well. Now, many years later, the famous Professor Mortimer is in charge of the British pavilion at the Brussels Universal Exposition. When strange phenomena begin disrupting preparations, Mortimer and his friend Blake set off on a trail that will take them to the sixth continent — to confront an old and unexpected enemy.

FEBRUARY 1958. SIMLA, THE FORMER SUMMER CAPITAL OF THE GOVERNMENT OF BRITISH INDIA, STANDS WITNESS TO A COLONIAL PAST THAT ITS INHABITANTS ARE STILL TRYING TO FORGET. IT SEEMS TO REAR UP ON THE FOOTHILLS OF THE HIMALAYAS, AS IF BETTER TO DEFY THE NEW SNOWS THAT ASSAIL IT.

THAT EVENING, AN UNUSUAL HUSTLE AND BUSTLE REIGNS AROUND THE FORMER VICEROY'S PALACE...

... THAT ISN'T ESCAPING NOTICE DESPITE THE LATE HOUR.

Do you see this, Lieutenant? Half of India's Maharajas must be gathered here!?

Our intelligence agents were not mistaken... This gathering is quite ominous. It's urgent we go have a look at what's happening behind these walls!

I'm ready, Lieutenant. Trust me: I'll bring back all the information you need.

You can go, my boy. But do be careful...

THE SARCOPHAGI OF THE SIXTH CONTINENT - Part 1

Edgard Félix Pierre Jacobs (1904–1987), better known under his pen name Edgar P. Jacobs, was a comic book creator (writer and artist), born in Brussels, Belgium. It has been said of Jacobs that he didn't remember a time when he hadn't drawn.

Jacobs assisted fellow Belgian Hergé (Georges Prosper Remi) in the recasting of Hergé's *Tintin in the Congo, Tintin in America, King Ottokar's Sceptre* and *The Blue Lotus* for book publication. He also contributed directly to both the drawing and storylines for the Tintin double-albums *The Secret of the Unicorn/Red Rackham's Treasure* and *The Seven Crystal Balls/Prisoners of the Sun.*

When the comics magazine Tintin was launched on 26th September 1946, it included Jacobs' story *Le secret de l'Espadon* (*The Secret of the Swordfish*). This story would be the first in the Blake and Mortimer series.

The characters of Captain Francis Blake, dashing head of MI5, his friend Professor Philip Mortimer, a nuclear physicist, and their sworn enemy Colonel Olrik became legendary heroes of the 9th art in the long-running series.

After Jacobs' death in 1987, Bob de Moor completed his unfinished last story. In the mid-1990s, the series was continued by the Jacobs Studios with new teams of writers and artists.

ORIGINAL FRENCH EDITION		
1	1950	Le secret de l'Espadon, T1
2	1953	Le secret de l'Espadon, T2
3	1953	Le secret de l'Espadon, T3
4	1954	Le mystère de la Grande Pyramide, T1
5	1955	Le mystère de la Grande Pyramide, T2
6	1956	La marque Jaune
7	1957	L'énigme de l'Atlantide
8	1959	S.O.S. Météores
9	1962	Le piège diabolique
10	1967	L'affaire du collier
11	1971	Les trois formules du professeur Satō, T1
12	1990	Les trois formules du professeur Satō, T2 (Jacobs/De Moor)
13	1996	L'affaire Francis Blake (Van Hamme/Benoit)
14	2000	La machination Voronov (Sente/Juillard)
15	2001	L'étrange rendez-vous (Van Hamme/Benoit)
16	2003	Les sarcophages du Sixième Continent, T1 (Sente/Juillard)
17	2004	Les sarcophages du Sixième Continent, T2 (Sente/Juillard)
18	2008	Le sanctuaire du Gondwana (Sente/Juillard)
19	2009	La malédiction des 30 deniers, T1 (Van Hamme/Sterne/De Spiegeleer)
20	2010	La malédiction des 30 deniers, T2 (Van Hamme/Aubin)
21	2012	Le serment des cinq Lords (Sente/Juillard)
22	2013	L'onde Septimus (Dufaux/Aubin/Schréder)
23	2014	Le bâton de Plutarque (Sente/Juillard)
24	2016	Le Testament de William S. (Sente/Juillard)

CINEBOOK EDITION		
15	2013	The Secret of the Swordfish, Part 1
16	2013	The Secret of the Swordfish, Part 2
17	2013	The Secret of the Swordfish, Part 3
2	2007	The Mystery of the Great Pyramid, Part 1
3	2008	The Mystery of the Great Pyramid, Part 2
1	2007	The Yellow "M"
12	2012	Atlantis Mystery
6	2009	S.O.S. Meteors
19	2014	The Time Trap
7	2010	The Affair of the Necklace
22	2016	Professor Satō's Three Formulae, Part 1
23	2016	Professor Satō's Three Formulae, Part 2
4	2008	The Francis Blake Affair
8	2010	The Voronov Plot
5	2009	The Strange Encounter
9	2011	The Sarcophagi of the Sixth Continent, Part 1
10	2011	The Sarcophagi of the Sixth Continent, Part 2
11	2011	The Gondwana Shrine
13	2012	The Curse of the 30 Pieces of Silver, Part 1
14	2012	The Curse of the 30 Pieces of Silver, Part 2
18	2014	The Oath of the Five Lords
20	2015	The Septimus Wave
21	2015	Plutarch's Staff
24	2016	The Testament of William S.